Rosalynn

Rosalynn

by Howard Norton

LOGOS INTERNATIONAL
Plainfield, New Jersey

Extract from a *Newsweek* interview on pp. 91-93 copyright 1977 by
Newsweek, Inc. All rights reserved. Reprinted by permission.

to my mother,
Grace Norton Murphey
and my wife,
Marjorie
for their faith, help
and encouragement

Table of Contents

Introduction

Rosalynn Carter is a different kind of first lady.

What she is doing goes far beyond the usual decorative functions of a White House hostess and sponsor of worthy charities.

She may, in fact, be recorded in history as the first presidential wife to have the political sensitivity and experience, and the knowledge of government to qualify for the unique role she is now playing, as the president's closest confidante and aide in many substantive affairs of state.

While the president is literally trapped in the Oval Office much of the time, because of the endless decisions that only he can make, the first lady is relatively free to move about. So, in effect, she has become an extension of the president's eyes and ears and mind, relaying to him the mood of the American people and of leaders and peoples overseas.

She is an established and important, though unofficial, part of the presidential team.

The president himself describes her role this way: "There's very seldom a decision that I make that I don't first discuss with her—either to tell her after the fact what I have done or, very frequently, to tell her my options and seek her advice.

"She's got superb political judgment. She probably knows the human aspects of the American people and their relationship to the government better than I do. We have an absolutely unconstrained relationship, an ability to express our doubts and concerns to each other."

To have this close relationship with his lifetime partner in the quiet hours at home must, indeed, be a blessing to the man who holds the highest and "the loneliest" job in the world.

Howard Norton
September, 1977

Rosalynn

1

The First Lady

It was 11:55 A.M. on Thursday, January 20, 1977.

Rosalynn Carter, hatless and wearing a green wool coat and matching scarf, sat in the chill wind on the inaugural platform, just to the left of the rostrum. Ranged in the rows around and behind her were the famous and the powerful of America. In exactly nine minutes her husband of thirty-one years, Jimmy Carter, would take the oath of office that would make him the thirty-ninth president of the United States. A sea of faces, spread across the Capitol's East Front parking plaza, watched her as the final moments of waiting ticked away.

Her face showed no expression. Her wide-set, intelligent eyes seemed to be fixed on something above and beyond the heads of the crowd, in the direction of the marbled halls of the Supreme Court. She sat, a little stiffly, grasping in her gloved hands the well-thumbed Bible that would be used to solemnize the oath. One of her fingers firmly marked the text, Micah 6:8, that would be the keynote of the president's inaugural speech.

There was a hushed murmur of conversation from the VIP seats close to the speaker's stand and the press area.

"Just look at her," a male voice said in a stage whisper. "She's got ice water in her veins!"

"Yeah," another voice agreed. "She's one tough lady. I hear this presidential thing was her idea in the first place, and she argued him into it, and then kept pushing till he made it."

"These soft-looking southern women, they can fool you," someone else put in. "Soft on the outside, solid steel inside. She ought to be nervous, but she just looks bored."

A woman's voice interrupted. "You can't tell me she isn't nervous. I say that nobody—man or woman—could sit where she is and face what she is facing and not be scared to death and trembling inside."

Aw, this is old stuff to her," another voice answered. "These political wives, they're in crowds, looking at crowds and talking to crowds all the time. I'll bet she's got something else on her mind. The way she's looking off into space, she's probably wondering about where she packed the shoes for tonight's parties."

From a press row seat nearby I watched that calm, handsome, deceptively young-looking face and as the whispered comments swirled around me I remembered an incident that happened during the Maryland primary campaign.

It was Sunday, a hot spring day—unusually hot even for Baltimore—just two days before Carter's jarring defeat by Governor Brown of California. Mrs. Carter, accompanied by only two campaign workers, had spent hours making drop-in visits to black churches in the northwestern part of the city. I had been trailing along, hoping for an interview.

It was well past one o'clock when she finally made her exit from the last scheduled visit, and started down the steps of the Gillies Memorial Church on Park Heights Avenue. I was following close behind, and heard her say something about being thirsty. This looked like my chance, so I blurted out, "Mrs. Carter, I'd like to buy you a Coke and take you to lunch." And as she looked around toward me, I explained: "I'm Washington correspondent for the *National Courier*, a Christian newspaper, and your headquarters told me I might get a chance to talk to you if I trailed along. Maybe we could talk at lunch?"

She offered me her hand and smiled, and turned back questioningly toward her companions.

"Well—I really don't know what our plans are for lunch, or maybe we haven't got time for lunch."

"Oh yes, you ought to have something to eat," the young woman aide said quickly. And then, turning to the youth who was doing the driving, she asked if he knew what the plans were.

He shook his head, and indicated he didn't think there were any plans, but added that it seemed like a good time to eat.

"Well," I pressed on, "if you'd like a nice, quiet, cool restaurant that looks like it might have good food, too, I know where 'we' can go," verbally attaching myself to the party with that word "we." "I just cased the place an hour ago, and I took the liberty of making reservations for four for 1:30."

The future first lady gave a helpless sort of shrug and shot a quizzical look at the others. "I guess it would be all right," she said. "Do you have a car, or would you like to ride with us?"

"I have my car here," I said. "Just follow me."

It was that first face-to-face meeting with Mrs.

Carter, nine months earlier, that flashed through my mind as I watched the soon-to-be first lady from my seat in the inaugural press area that cold January morning.

As she had sipped a glass of iced tea and nibbled at a salad, while a dozen or so black customers at other tables strained to hear, she had frankly confessed to me that self-confidence was one of her weakest points, and that fear of doing or saying the wrong things had been a major problem all her life.

"Then how did you overcome it?" I asked. "You certainly seemed to be at ease all day today."

Smiling her thanks, she explained it this way. "I never made speeches until Jimmy was governor. I didn't think I could do anything like that.

"Then, one day, somebody sent me this little tract. It was titled: 'Lovingly in the Hands of the Father,' and it said that if you put yourself at all times completely in the hands of the Lord, he will take care of you all the time, and you can go ahead and do anything you have to do.

"So I found that I could get up and stand in front of those crowds, and think to myself, 'I'm lovingly in the hands of the Father,' and then I could look them right in the eyes and talk to them and not be afraid that I was doing it wrong or of what they might think of me."

After a pause, she added: "You know, I think Jimmy does the same thing. You may not think so, but he's a very private man, maybe what you'd call an introvert. He's really quite shy, down deep inside.

"One day, I remember, I told him I was worried about what I was saying in the radio interviews. I was afraid I'd say something that would hurt him; something that would not come out the way he would answer it.

"But Jimmy just looked at me with sort of a frown, and said: 'Don't you pray before you go on the air? Don't you pray when you find out you are going to be asked to go on the air? Don't you pray "God help me, God help me"?'

"I told him yes, I did. 'Then that's all that's necessary,' he said. 'You just ask the Lord to help you do the best you can, and you'll do all right.'

"I know that's the way he does it. He does the best job he possibly can do, then turns it over to the Lord. That's all we can do."

Thinking back over that chat with Mrs. Carter as I watched her on inauguration day morning I felt a warm glow of understanding and sympathy for this beautiful lady, so few years removed from her life as a small-town girl in southwestern Georgia.

I felt that we shared a secret the others in this vast crowd did not and could not know; the secret that not one victory, but two, were being celebrated there that day: The new president's victory in the election, of course, but also his wife's victory over self and over fear, through her faith in the Lord Jesus Christ.

The hour finally arrived. The two presidents, the old and the new, walked onto the platform. There was a resounding cheer and a long round of applause. In just a moment, now, Rosalynn Carter would rise and stand facing this vast crowd, between her husband and the chief justice, holding the Bible while the new president took his oath.

I glanced at her one more time as she sat there. Her face was still solemn and expressionless. But I was sure that I knew what was passing through her mind at that moment. She was almost certainly telling the small-town Rosalynn, deep inside, that she was "lovingly in the hands of the Father." And after that, a poised and gracious first lady, she would rise from her chair and stand, without fear, before the eyes of the world.

Things were radically different, for Rosalynn, when her husband won the governorship of Georgia, on his second try, in 1970.

Friends and relatives in Plains described her then as "tense and frightened" at the prospect of having to take over the social duties at the governor's mansion in sophisticated Atlanta.

Despite her husband's encouragement and support, she confided to friends that she was "constantly worried."

"I had the idea that a governor's wife must be perfect," she said years later. "I just *knew* that people would be watching me, and that my clothes, hair, nails, conversation and manners all had to be exactly right. But I know myself pretty well. I felt shy, awkward and inadequate. The very idea of making a speech made me physically sick."

Her social experience, up to that time, had centered in Plains and Americus, and she had never faced the problems of finger bowls, servants and the pitfalls and dangers of seating by protocol at her dinners.

Her friends in Plains and Americus couldn't help her, and she resolved firmly that she was not going to display her ignorance of high society by confiding in someone with a background of Atlanta aristocracy. Her husband's repeated assurances made her feel better, but only for a little while.

She says now that even Amy, who was then three years old, was suffering from Rosalynn's effort to attain perfection. "I drove myself nearly crazy trying to keep her perfect, in clothes and everything else," she now admits.

All during the campaign for the governorship,

Rosalynn had motored over the state and campaigned on the issues. And all during the election campaign she had looked forward eagerly to taking an active part in the governor's administration as an active solver of social problems, not primarily as the governor's social hostess.

So she finally decided to do what she now acknowledged she should have done many months earlier: she got on her knees and told the Lord about her worries and difficulties.

"You just can't live that way," she says now. "You can't be worried and tense all the time, and still be friendly with people, and get your jobs done, too."

Rosalynn had hand-picked the jobs she wanted to do long before the ballots were cast in that 1970 Georgia election. She wanted to help reform Georgia's state mental health organization. And she had ideas of her own about the state's loosely knit and excessively expensive and inefficient government organization. With these things on her mind, she grew impatient over the prospective demands of social life in the governor's mansion.

Looking back now, some of her Christian friends say they believe the Lord moved Jimmy Carter into the governor's mansion in Atlanta so that she and Jimmy would not have to start their education from scratch when they moved into the

9

White House in Washington.

Whether they are right or wrong, that's the way it worked out. Rosalynn's prayers were answered. Her striving toward perfectionism diminished.

One of her closest friends in Plains confided to me that Rosalynn had told her what the Lord's advice had been when she prayed over the problems of the governor's mansion.

"His advice," she said, "was to be herself. Just to be Rosalynn Carter of Plains, Georgia, and to live that life the best way she could. And if she needed help, to come back, again, in prayer, and ask for it."

That was the turning point, the start of Rosalynn Carter's liberal education in both politics and social matters.

Her friends sum it up this way. "She came to terms with her looks, and learned, to her surprise, that many of her friends were admirers of her beautifully wrinkle-free face, and her large liquid brown eyes.

"She accepted the fact that she was not gifted with the ability to make dazzling small talk, but found that people were not bored when she poured out her enthusiasm for better mental health programs, and her dismay at the long delays in bringing help to the aged 'who haven't got time to wait for it.'

"She gave up her search for perfection, and found that imperfection, seasoned with love, compassion and understanding can be more effective."

Charles Kirbo, the sixty-year-old Atlanta lawyer who is the Carter family's most trusted political adviser and an intimate friend of both Jimmy and Rosalynn, gave this description of the Rosalynn Carter metamorphosis. "I've really enjoyed watching her grow and develop from the very timid person she was when I first met her. At the outset, she didn't want any part of political fund-raising. She would say flatly 'No, I can't do it. You forget it.' It was amazing to see her get bold enough to ask for money. And she really got good at it, and at almost everything else in the political arena.

"You Washington people are going to find that she has very good taste, and she'll do a good job of running the White House. But she'll not do a lot of entertaining. She will, however, have a lot of people in to see the White House. And wine will probably be the strongest liquor served while she's in charge."

Now and then, the president and first lady have been known to disagree publicly. Once during the campaign, Carter told a questioner that his wife was opposed to Women's Lib. The next day Rosalynn read it in the newspaper and told reporters publicly, and firmly, that he had made a mistake.

Another close Carter friend, Philip Alston, Jr., an Atlanta lawyer, confides that in the early days of Carter's governorship, "you could see Rosalynn growing before your very eyes."

"It was remarkable," he says. "When the years in the governor's mansion ended Rosalynn was given high marks by those who watched her learn, and accomodate to public life.

"She and Jimmy are very close. They have a relationship that is a deeply moving thing, when you see it. It's one of the few great love affairs I've seen in my lifetime. They manage to be in love, and still remain friends. And they do another remarkable thing as man and wife—they seek each other's advice, and quite frequently accept it."

A veteran professional member of the White House staff, who has served under three other presidents says the country is fortunate, indeed, that this first lady does not need on-the-job training.

She let it be known from the start, he says, that the Carters are not going to change their style of living, just because they are living in the White House.

Although they seldom have a family breakfast or lunch, Rosalynn asks that they all do their best to come to the family dinners. And she has told her friends that her greatest domestic role for the next four to eight years will be to hold the family together, both for the family's sake, and as an example of happy family life to Americans, and to all the world.

Although her need for perfection is gone, Rosalynn said she finds it hard to relax. There are so many things she wants to do.

"If I sit down to watch television, I have to have something in my hands," she says. "I feel I have to be doing something every minute. I wish I could relax like Jimmy. He works hard and long hours, but when he stops working he puts it out of his mind and really stops."

Apparently as part of her program to keep her hands busy, First Lady Rosalynn brought her sewing machine to the White House from Plains. She does some of her own mending, and makes an occasional dress or play clothes for Amy, just as she has always done at home in Plains, or even in the Atlanta years, when Carter was governor.

One of her friends recently asked her why it was she felt it necessary to build a tree house for Amy right in the midst of the formal gardens that border the White House south lawn; a tree house that had to be just like the one Amy had in Plains.

Rosalynn's reply gave a key to her philosophy of life. "Some things," she said, "should remain constant."

2

The Smiths

The best way to tell you about "Miss" Allie Smith is to tell you about the time her son, Murray, was divorced by his wife, Frances.

Now divorce is not all that common in Plains, Georgia, because life there centers around churches—the Baptist and the Methodist mainly—and these are people who take literally and seriously the warning that no man should "put asunder" any married couple "whom God hath joined together."

So, while her neighbors and friends say she didn't show it, and didn't say a single word about it, it must have been a shock to "Miss" Allie and it must have been a very deep hurt, to have this happen in her family. But to an outsider trying to figure out what makes the people of Plains what

15

they are, the thing that is a lot more surprising than "Miss" Allie's calm acceptance of this domestic tragedy is her apparent decision to ignore it.

Everyone in Plains will tell you that it didn't make a bit of difference in her relationship with now ex-daughter-in-law, Frances Smith. She just kept on mothering, protecting and socializing with the young lady as if nothing had happened.

Frances, herself, openly confesses her love for her former mother-in-law, and sees nothing surprising in their continued relationship because, as she says, she knows "Miss" Allie pretty well—has known her most of her life. And the people of Plains just shrug and tell you it's no big thing, for the same reason.

But just among themselves, and when they're not talking to an outsider, a stranger, who is poking around town with a notebook, asking questions, they must know, and admit, they've got a very unusual lady in their midst in the person of "Miss" Allie Smith. They do read the Atlanta papers, so it should be clear to them that the way the seventy-one-year-old Widow Smith continues to mother and protect and socialize with the girl who divorced her son just isn't the way things happen in the real world, outside of Plains.

"Of all the people in the world I didn't want to hurt, it was Mother Allie Smith," Frances told an inquiring reporter. "I know the divorce hurt her

16

but she has never uttered a single word of criticism to me, and nobody has ever told me of anything like that she has ever said to them about me.

"Those people who make up the jokes about mothers-in-law should meet mother. I still call her "mother," because she still treats me like a daughter.

"She knows I simply love rutabagas, and when she cooks up a batch she calls me to come over and eat with her. If I have a problem I go to her and tell her about it, and she always will try to do what she can to help. It gives me a feeling of comfort and security to know that Mother Smith is just down the street."

Murray, the other half of the broken family, has a master's degree in science and teaches math and science in high school. When he and Frances were divorced, about three years ago, he went home to live with his mother. He was forty-two at the time and "Miss" Allie hadn't had to "do" for a family for some years, but he says she stepped right into the routine of "preparing my meals and washing my clothes." And she still washes clothes for him, even though he has now moved to his own place.

I'm telling you all this because this same "Miss" Allie is the mother of Rosalynn Carter, the current first lady of the United States. And the people who have known them both for many years declare that the mother and daughter are as identical in their outlook on life as any mother and daughter anywhere could possibly be.

The words they use to describe the mother of the first lady—the mother they say is so much like the first lady—are "generous," "kind," "understanding," "quiet," "independent," "hard-working" and "determined," once she makes up her mind that something has to be done.

They will tell you, in Plains, that Jimmy Carter says he owes his winning of the presidency, in part, at least, to the way Mother Allie Smith brought up her daughter, Rosalynn. They say he credits her mother with instilling in Rosalynn the qualities which made her such a determined campaigner. And they add that the president says "Miss" Allie could have campaigned in Rosalynn's place if she had been the same age, and had been faced with the same sudden need to throw off her inborn shyness and go out and face the public.

The first lady herself is said to describe her mother as an "extraordinary" person, gentle but firm with her four children after the death of her husband, Edgar, when "Miss" Allie was only thirty-four-years-old.

"We depended on mother for everything after father died," Rosalynn says. "And that's when I saw my mother develop into a strong, independent person, assuming full responsibility for the family, and asking no help or charity from anyone. This made a deep impression on me. I'm sure it turned out to be a permanent influence."

Son Murray says his Methodist mother's personal demonstration of Christianity in her life, and her insistence that the children go to Sunday school and church and study the Bible regularly gave all of the children a religious foundation that remains with them to this day. "Church was, and still is, a must, a central activity in all our lives."

Murray himself is a Methodist lay speaker who, on occasion, fills the pulpit when the regular pastor is out of town. And, like his brother-in-law, Jimmy Carter, he teaches Sunday school regularly.

Murray acknowledges that he got some of his religion through the seat of his pants, "because I was a mischievous youngster, and it took a good peach-tree switch to impress on me what was right and what was wrong."

Murray's brother, Jerry, has a degree in engineering and lives in Indiana where he works for a steel company.

The first lady's sister, Alethea, is a graduate of Georgia Southwestern College, and has worked in banks in Americus, Georgia and Atlanta.

Jerry tells this story about his mother. She used psychology on them, he says. She had to be both father and mother to her brood, and when they started dating she would not lay down any deadline time for returning home. Most of the other kids told the Smith children their parents did set a time limit. But instead of limiting their evening social activities, "Miss" Allie "repeatedly impressed on us that she had tried, all our lives, to teach us what is right and what is wrong, and that if we hadn't learned that by then, she had failed as a mother.

"Well, after a quiet lecture like that we all went out with our dates determined that we would do the right thing so mother would not feel she had failed. And we almost always got home at a reasonable hour."

The neighbors say it wasn't for lack of opportunity that "Miss" Allie never remarried, after leukemia took the life of her husband. They report that one persistent suitor kept on bringing candy and flowers for about ten years before deciding it was hopeless.

She had frequently told her children that she could "never love another man." She had first met her husband, who was nine years older, when she was in the ninth grade and he was the driver of the school bus.

She went through high school in Plains, and after graduation went on to the Georgia State College for Women to study home economics before she married Edgar Smith who, by then, was the town mechanic and was also farming on land that he owned.

When Edgar died, he left a small inheritance to his family, but Rosalynn has told interviewers that her mother resolved not to touch the inheritance, and to bring up and educate her children by her own efforts.

Mrs. Smith enjoyed sewing, so she turned to sewing as a means of making a living. She made all kinds of dresses on order, even wedding dresses which, later, became a specialty. And she even branched out into tailoring men's suits and overcoats.

She remembers now that when she started tailoring, in 1940, a man's coat cost about four or five dollars, but she admits she might not have charged enough for the work, in her eagerness to get enough orders to keep the family going.

Rosalynn, the oldest of the four children, was the first to go to work. She took a job washing hair at a local beauty shop, and at home she helped with the younger children. And as Rosalynn took over more and more responsiblility in the family she and her mother grew very close, she says.

Jerry was eleven, Murray eight, Alethea three and Rosalynn was thirteen at the time of their father's death. Mrs. Smith rented the family farm, but insisted on putting the rent proceeds into savings so her children could go to college when the time came. Later, she took a civil service examination and was awarded a job as assistant to the postmaster in Plains, a job that she kept continuouly until she reached the mandatory retirement age of seventy.

The independent "Miss" Allie was reported to

have displayed the nearest thing to bitterness that anyone had seen through all her years, when she was told that, even though she was healthy and alert, she had to retire because that was the way the law said it had to be.

But "Miss" Allie hasn't yet really given up the urge to work. When Rosalynn and Jimmy moved to Washington she scanned the employment prospects in booming Plains and took a part-time job at a flower shop. That left her enough spare time to work a few hours a week at the Plains railroad station, now converted into a Jimmy Carter souvenir shop.

She also found time, later, to join 379 other Georgians on a people-to-people flight to England—the first of what Jimmy and Rosalynn Carter hope will be a continuing series of "Friendship Force" flights between the individual American States and friendly foreign countries. It was her very first trip outside the United States. And she agreed to go, she told reporters, because Jimmy had promised the friendly people of Newcastle-on-Tyne that a genuine member of the Carter clan would be on board the first friendship flight to their city. And that is where "Miss" Allie got her initial look at England.

That experience in her mother's life, according to Rosalynn, gave her the incentive to take over the cause of bringing justice and fairness to the treatment of the elderly, after Jimmy won the presidency. That, and her commitment to the improvement of mental health facilities and furthering of public education to improve the understanding of mental health problems are her top-priority jobs, by her own choice.

Allie Smith—Allie Murray before she married—was an only child in a family that loved children and wanted more of them. The first lady compares the sheltered and loving treatment her mother got in her childhood to the way the Carters now adore and shelter their ten-year-old Amy.

Allie's father, the combination farmer and Botsford postmaster known to all his friends as "The Captain," was a deeply religious man, and was a great influence on her early life, an influence that clearly has followed her to this day.

She recalls that he was strict, almost fanatical about "observing the sabbath day to keep it holy. He didn't believe in doing anything on Sunday," she says. "He wanted me to just sit and learn verses, while he read his Bible."

He was also a firm believer in the theory that the best way to teach is by example. The story that she tells to illustrate this, she has related to many interviewers. She regards it as the key to her father's character.

It seems that her father was plowing one day on the family farm, and that Allie, a very small child at the time, was playing in the plowed furrows behind him. At one point, for reasons only known to the mules, they simply stopped and refused to go another step.

"Doggone!" her father blurted out, as he slapped the bottoms of the troublesome beasts and jerked the reins.

"I was right behind him, and I heard his exclamation, so I copied him and repeated 'Doggone!' before he got the mules started again," "Miss" Allie says.

Her father whirled and looked at her with a shocked expression on his face when he realized what she had said. "He never said a word to me about it, but the look he gave me was enough to tell me that he felt he had failed, in this instance, to set the good example that he had set as his lifetime goal as a Christian."

"I never heard him use that expression again," she declares.

Mrs. Smith makes it obvious that she is proud of all her children, and when you question her about her famous daughter in the White House, she is likely to turn the conversation and say something nice about one of the others.

She's also reported to be an "easy mark" for her twelve grandchildren. Nobody has ever heard her raise her voice at any of them. And they learned quickly that if they wanted some little thing their parents were refusing to buy for them, Mother Allie was almost certain to come through with the needed funds.

Rosalynn and her mother continue to enjoy the closest possible mother-daughter relationship. Even during the presidential campaign they used to get together to sew and cook, or to shop at the stores in Americus, as often as Rosalynn could take the time out of her intensive speaking schedule.

Rosalynn makes no secret of the fact she misses this togetherness with her mother, now that she has moved into the White House and the trips to Plains grow more and more infrequent. And she has expressed the hope that her mother will not feel too uncomfortable when she visits the family in the White House, so she will be willing to come often.

Mrs. Smith, though she glows with pride in Rosalynn and Jimmy, seems to have mixed feelings about their new life in the national and world spotlight.

She has fears about what the lack of privacy is going to do to her grandchildren and great-grandchildren. And the legion of secret service agents who follow the family everywhere are a constant reminder to her of the real physical danger that goes along with the job of president.

As to Amy, Grandmother Allie's greatest regret is that she may never again get a chance to be "just an ordinary little girl."

"I pray constantly for them all," she says.

There have been some major changes in the life
of Allie Smith, herself, since her daughter moved
away.

There's an empty rocking chair now on the
front porch of her gray clapboard house, just four
houses down the street from the Carter
Warehouse. "Miss" Allie used to like to sit in that
chair in the cool of the afternoon and evening and
greet friends and neighbors as they walked by or
drove past on their way to or from the Plains
shopping area.

She doesn't do it any more, because on many
days the traffic is almost bumper-to-bumper and
the faces that peer at her out of the cars are the
faces of tourists, just like the faces in the Plains
tour bus when it passes and when the driver
announces that "on your right is the home of Mrs.
Carter's mother, 'Miss' Allie Smith. It was in this
house that. . . ."

"It's just like they write about the Hollywood
stars," according to the neighbors. " 'Miss' Allie
has just been driven inside her own home to get
some privacy."

Also, she had to have her telephone number
changed to one not listed in the phone book. She
gives it only to old friends.

They say she avoids having her photograph
taken, because she wants, at least, to be able to
walk through her own hometown without being
recognized by the tourists.

"Miss" Allie went to Washington for the

inauguration and, according to whispered information from the first lady's press office, she slept in the Lincoln bedroom and slept soundly after that hectic first day, in spite of the family's tongue-in-cheek warning that the ghost of Lincoln himself has been known to hover over the bed on occasion.

And when she went back home to Plains, her friends say, there were several days when she was in low spirits; not because she missed the excitement of the capital, but because she knew she could never again have that comfortable, family feeling of being able, on the spur of the moment, to get in her car and drive the few blocks to the Carters' for a visit with Rosalynn and Amy.

But her closest friends in Plains are sure that mood will not last long; that would not be in character for "Miss" Allie.

She has her friends, she has her church, she has her Bible. In her quiet moments she must also have deep pride in the knowledge that her daughter lives in the White House and is openly acknowledged by the president, her son-in-law, to be the one who is his closest adviser.

Already, Rosalynn Smith Carter has stepped easily and naturally into a position of influence and power that no other first lady ever attained.

And, as the daughter of "Miss" Allie Smith, of Plains, Georgia she is not likely to forget the source of that power.

3

The Beginning

So far as anybody knows, the only lasting disagreement between President and Mrs. Carter—the only thing on which they still, to this day, disagree—is the story of how it all began; the story of how the romance between Rosalynn Smith and Jimmy Carter got started.

As the president tells it, the whole thing from the start was his idea. But Rosalynn tells all her interviewers that she had to use a considerable amount of feminine guile to get him even to look at her. Carter was a sophisticated Annapolis midshipman at the time. He was three years older than she was and not at all interested in girls who were so young, she says.

But there is also a third version, the one being told by the president's mother, "Miss" Lillian, and to my ear it has more of the ring of disinterested truth and accurate recollection than either of the others. She told me her version of the story when I visited her at her now-famous "pond house," near Plains, in the spring of 1976.

She spoke warmly of her daughter-in-law. "Rosalynn was my daughter Ruth's best friend, always," she said. "And Rosalynn was at my house almost every weekend in those days, or if she wasn't there with us, Ruth was in Plains spending the weekend with Rosalynn. That is the kind of close friendship it was. And it continues to this day.

"Well, they were high school girls, and Jimmy had already been in college for two years before he got his appointment to Annapolis. He was at Georgia Southwestern for the 1941-42 school year, and then he went to Georgia Tech the next school year, all the time hoping for the big break from Annapolis. It finally came, and he entered the Naval Academy in the 1943-44 term.

Finances were a little pinched in those days and, although Jimmy had a yen to try the navy as a career, he has always said that he was first attracted to the Naval Academy because the tuition was free.

"Well, now, to get back to the romance: When Jimmy came home from the Naval Academy for the first time he paid no attention to Rosalynn and Ruth. To him they were just kids. He would run into them sometimes in the kitchen, and he would just say, 'Hi, Ruth, Hi, Rosalynn,' and that was it.

"Well, one night, on one of his trips home from the academy, Jimmy and some of his friends decided to give a dance over here at the pond house. We had a sort of jukebox there, and they could make all the noise they wanted to, because we have no close neighbors, as you can see.

"It just happened that Ruth and Rosalynn were spending that weekend here with us.

"I don't know what it was that gave them the idea—maybe there was a temporary shortage of girls, or something—but the boys saw Ruth and Rosalynn here at the house and they said, in a sort of offhand way: 'Why don't you girls get somebody to bring you, and come and join the party.'

"Now you can imagine that no high school girl is going to pass up an invitation to go to a college boy's party. So that's what they did. They got dates—I don't remember who—and they went to the dance.

"Now the rest of this story I got in confidence in a kitchen-table talk with Rosalynn later," continued Miss Lillian.

"Jimmy danced first with Ruth and then with her—Rosalynn. And while he was dancing with her, Jimmy said to Rosalynn: 'Don't you think the date I brought is pretty?' And Rosalynn said she snapped right back at Jimmy: 'She's not half as pretty as I am!'

"Well, I think Jimmy must have taken a closer look at Rosalynn at that point, because it was only a few days later that he came into the kitchen and said: 'Mother, do you know who I have a date with tonight?' And I said: 'Who?' And he said: 'Rosalynn.' And they began to date just about every night after that, when he came home from Annapolis. And I don't think he ever again dated anyone else.

"Rosalynn tells me that she had a crush on Jimmy for two years before he got around to asking her for a date."

Now as the president tells it, the story started off in a different way, but eventually gets around to the same steady dating.

He says that he and a friend were driving around Plains in the friend's car—a rumble-seat Ford—"when we happened to see my sister Ruth and another girl in the churchyard. So we stopped to talk to them, and the other girl was Rosalynn, who was Ruth's closest friend. And I think we finally asked them if they'd like to go to the movies, and they said 'yes' and that was my first date with Rosalynn."

The president insists that he told his mother, before he left Plains from that visit home, that he was in love with Rosalynn and wanted to marry her.

And after he got back to school he says he wrote

to Rosalynn every other day, and she wrote to him about as often. And when he came home at Christmas he proposed to her and she turned him down. He says she told him she didn't know, for sure, yet, what she wanted in life.

But Rosalynn didn't take long to decide what she wanted. When Jimmy came home from the academy for the Washington's Birthday break, they became engaged.

Rosalynn recalls the events that led up to the engagement somewhat differently.

She and Jimmy have known each other all their lives. Their families were so close that when Rosalynn's father—who was the town mechanic—became ill with leukemia and died, when Rosalynn was thirteen years old, Jimmy's mother, "Miss" Lillian, a registered nurse, took care of the dying man. And on the day he died, "Miss" Lillian brought the grieving Rosalynn back to her own home to spend the night with Ruth.

After that, the first lady now recalls, she saw Jimmy at school, at the drug store and often at Magnolia Springs, where there was a dance pavilion and a place to swim. She says that she wasn't much impressed with the man who eventually became her husband until the summer of 1945, the year before they were married.

"The snappy white uniform he wore that summer might have had something to do with it," she says.

Whatever it was, Rosalynn now confesses that she developed "quite a crush" on the vacationing midshipman, and set to work to find ways to attract his attention.

"Finally," as she tells it, "only two days before Jimmy was to return to Annapolis for his senior year, Ruth and Rosalynn volunteered to help Jimmy clean the pond house, and it must have worked.

"We just slaved all day," she says, "and then I went to the Methodist Youth Fellowship at the church. After supper, Ruth and her date came by, and Jimmy was sitting in the rumble seat. He got out of the car and asked me if I'd go to a movie with him. I was so excited! It was wonderful! He was older, and *so* good-looking. But I don't know what made me fall in love with him. I don't remember. I just loved him, that's all."

As a token of their engagement, Jimmy gave her the traditional scaled-down version of the Naval Academy ring. They were married on July 7th, 1946, after his graduation, in the Plains Methodist Church. The Smiths were always Methodists, but Rosalynn changed denominations when she changed her name. She has been a Baptist ever since.

Rosalynn's mother, Allie Murray Smith, widowed in 1941, is a shy, practical, resourceful woman whose wide-set eyes and delicately handsome face were obviously inherited by her daughter.

After the death of her husband, Mrs. Smith made a business for herself sewing wedding dresses for the town's brides, and later she worked in the post office to keep her family in clothing and food. She managed so well that when it came time for Rosalynn to go to college, there was enough money to cover the cost. Some of the cost was paid by Rosalynn herself, from money earned as a teen-ager when she worked in the local beauty parlor, shampooing the hair of the ladies of the town. She was seventeen when she enrolled in Georgia Southwestern Junior College in nearby Americus. She majored in interior decorating. But her college career was cut short two years later by her marriage to Jimmy Carter.

Her friends in Plains recall that Rosalynn was an unusually neat, clean child. When she was little, they say, she seemed always to wear a big taffeta bow in her curly hair and a clean dress that almost never was dirtied, wherever she played.

Later, she moved up into pigtails and a bicycle, and spent much of her time helping her mother do her commercial sewing. Rosalynn was the oldest of the four Smith children, so there was a lot of baby-sitting to be done, too, with her brothers,

Jerry and Murray, and her baby sister Alethea.

Always healthy and active, the future first lady is recalled as an enthusiastic basketball player. Her friends and neighbors in Plains say she was "just a typical, busy, intelligent child, who did all the things that the others were doing."

She read a lot of books, got reasonably good grades in school, listened to "Hit Parade" on the radio, squealed with all the other girls at Frank Sinatra movies, and learned to jitterbug. Like most of the others of her age she "hung out" a lot at the local drug store.

In contrast with the childhood of her husband, who was brought up on the Carter farm at Archer, just a few miles outside Plains, Rosalynn was a "town girl." But she says now that some of the happiest days of her childhood were in the summers when she spent weekends or a couple of weeks at the farm of her maternal grandfather, whom everyone called "Captain Murray" or simply, "The Captain."

Murray was postmaster at Botsford, five miles down the road from Plains, and he also operated a farm, growing peanuts and cotton.

It was on the Murray farm that Rosalynn was born. But her visits to the farm were not entirely for the opportunity of having fun in the country. She and her two brothers usually timed their visits to coincide with a harvest, and the three of them worked, stacking peanuts "at fifteen cents a pile" or picking cotton.

Part of these earnings always were saved, a habit that was acquired reluctantly, but which served them well when they reached college age. All four of Widow Smith's children got a college education, says Rosalynn, without touching the inheritance her father had left to take care of the family.

Both the town of Plains and the schools were segregated when Rosalynn and her brothers and sister were young. So it was only on their grandfather's farm that they came to know any blacks of their own age.

The first lady still remembers with pleasure the days when she played kick-ball with the black children of her grandfather's farm laborers, using a can instead of a ball. She was taught by the farm children to jump from the hayloft into the haystacks, to play hide-and-seek in the old barn, and to find the places where the wandering hens laid their eggs. It was a thoroughly happy time in her life, she says.

Following their marriage, Rosalynn and Jimmy plunged with enthusiasm into the life of a typical navy family.

"I loved those years," Rosalynn told a recent interviewer. "We were so close then. We studied books together. We listened to Rachmaninoff concertos and we memorized Shakespeare. We did so many things that we don't have time for any more."

The first Carter son, Jack (John William) was born while Jimmy was stationed in Portsmouth, Virginia.

Then came orders for Jimmy to go to submarine school in New London, Connecticut. And after that he and the family were shipped off for a glorious interlude in Honolulu, where he was assigned to the crew of a submarine.

That is how it happens that the second Carter son, "Chip" (James Earl III) is a native of Hawaii.

There was a brief assignment in San Diego before the family returned, again, to New London. And there the third son, "Jeff" (Jeffrey) was born in 1952.

Although Rosalynn looks back with pleasure on the navy days she acknowledges that life had its rough moments. She was alone much of the time, with her husband traveling or at sea. And she found that raising three small children without a husband in the house was tough work.

"But I was seeing the world for the first time. I was having a good time and I loved the travel," she says. "And that," she adds, "is why we had our first really violent disagreement in 1953, when Jimmy's father died of cancer and he felt obliged to abandon his navy career and go back to Plains to save the family peanut business and help his mother."

Rosalynn tells interviewers that she "screamed and yelled" her opposition to the change that her husband insisted on making. But finally she bowed out of the battle and reluctantly packed up and returned to the old hometown.

Then followed some years of hard work, for both of them.

After Jimmy resigned his commission, their only financial resources were savings bonds that they had squirreled away while they were with the navy. They applied for, and received, a minimum-rent public housing apartment in Plains, so they would have privacy and would not have to move in with either of their mothers.

In 1954, she says, their peanut business chalked up a total profit of two hundred dollars.

"Jimmy did the manual labor, and I kept the books and weighed the trucks and did most of the other office work," she recalls.

She continued to work full-time beside her husband to build up the fertilizer and seed business they had started to supplement the farm income. After school and on Saturdays their fast-growing family of boys pitched in and helped, too.

Their prosperity finally provided time to focus on the world outside the family business, and it was then that Jimmy found that the political "bug" he had inherited from his father, who had been a member of the Georgia legislature, was still alive and active.

He ran for the Georgia state senate and won—but only after a lawyer named Charles Kirbo, now a close presidential adviser, stepped to his side and won a court battle over some ballot-stuffing and other assorted corruption. For both Rosalynn and Jimmy, that race was their primary education in politics. Both of them campaigned hard.

Then came disaster.

The Carter team—Rosalynn and Jimmy—saw a chance to win the governorship in 1966. They entered the race on short notice, late in the campaign. They lost. Lester Maddox, the segregationist, won.

Deeply in debt, mentally depressed and possibly dead, politically, the Carters laid their problems before the Lord. It was their first experience with failure. But it was the beginning of their greatest success.

From the depths of his despair, Jimmy Carter once more opened his heart to the Holy Spirit and renewed his close personal relationship with the living God.

The rest is history. First came governorship. Then the presidency of the United States. And along with all of this, a special bonus: little Amy Carter, the daughter Rosalynn had always wanted.

4

The Housewife

For the first twenty-five years of her married life, Rosalynn Carter says, she got up near dawn every morning to prepare a nourishing breakfast for her early rising husband. She did this, she relates, at a sacrifice of her early-morning beauty sleep, which she loved. But, in a reverse twist that would have delighted O. Henry, she found out from her husband, after twenty-five years of this daily sacrifice, that he didn't like breakfast, and never had. All he really wanted, he said, was a glass of orange juice and a cup of coffee, and he could prepare that himself.

The moral of this story, according to the first lady, is that if you want to do something nice for your husband, be sure that it's something he really likes and appreciates, and not something he will silently put up with just to be nice to you.

But the first lady has good reasons not to hold any resentment because of her husband's years of silence on the subject of nourishing breakfasts, because it was Jimmy Carter who knew how to cook when they got married, and who continued to cook over the years, even during the campaign. He also gave his wife her first lessons in cooking, and she took to the art with such enthusiasm that she enrolled in a fancy cooking school in Atlanta and became the family expert.

But Jimmy continued to help, not only with the cooking but with everything else around the house, including the housecleaning, she says. She reveals this with a smile, knowing that it won't help to make him popular with the masculine voters.

One of the secrets of their thirty-one years of happy marriage, according to Mrs. Carter, is that "we have always done things as equals."

"We have never had household help," she says, "except in the governor's mansion in Atlanta, and now in the White House. Jimmy and I have always worked hard, and Jimmy's mother and my mother also worked hard, and never had any help."

The Carters enjoy entertaining at home in Plains, and she says a secret of good hospitality, one that always makes a party more enjoyable, is that "everything doesn't have to be perfect."

"Jimmy used to say to me when we had a party

coming up: 'You just do your best, and the rest will take care of itself.' That's especially good advice today when just about every woman I know works hard. Southern women are just like women everywhere else in this, trying to balance off the demands of a job against the real pleasures of having a home and sharing it with friends.

"They know that when they have people in, the house may not be perfectly straight, and the children aren't going to be perfectly neat. The only thing to do is just relax and make everyone else feel more comfortable."

The Carter family has lived in the vicinity of Plains for about two hundred years, so there's quite a crowd when they get together, and they get together often, Rosalynn says.

"When all of my family, and all of Jimmy's family and the boys and their wives get together we have some space problems," and the bigger the crowd the more informal the party gets.

"I can seat ten in the dining room," she says, "and six in the breakfast room and four in the den. But if there are twenty or more, we turn it into a buffet."

Cooking was one of the Carters' favorite forms of relaxation during the presidential campaign. Both of them would head for the kitchen, because, after all those airline and campaign meals, Jimmy just wanted fresh vegetables. His brother, Billy, always had a garden full of eggplant, zucchini and tomatoes. Jimmy, according to his wife, liked to experiment with eggplant dishes, all of which the president calls "goulash"—his term for casserole cooking.

"I never had to worry about what to cook because the neighbors—knowing how busy we were—kept us supplied with food. That's in the great tradition of Southern hospitality."

Although Rosalynn Carter is not a trained nutritionist, her mother, "Miss" Allie Smith, was a home economics major at the Georgia State College for Women, and Rosalynn got good training at home. "Mother," she says, "was always very careful to see that we ate right."

She says she has tried to follow the same rule with daughter Amy, but learned to her chagrin that Amy was allowed to snack on all sorts of sweets by her paternal grandmother, the president's mother, who was baby-sitter for the Carters during the campaign months. "Every time we got home the refrigerator was full of honeybuns, candy, doughnuts and a lot of other things we wouldn't allow in the house."

For other American mothers who may be having the same worries with candy-hungry children, Mrs. Carter has a solution. It's called "fruit candy" and she says it's now Amy's favorite—when Mrs. Carter has the time to prepare a batch. So here is the Rosalynn Carter recipe for "fruit candy":

Grind together ½ pound of dates, 1 pound of figs, 2 cups of chopped walnuts or pecans, ½ cup of seedless raisins, and 1 pound of dried apricots. Press into a buttered pan. Cut into squares and sprinkle each square with one teaspoon of grated orange zest or sesame seeds or unsweetened shredded coconut.

Mrs. Carter says they eat simple foods at home, and have continued the same custom at the White House. And she has always given special attention to providing a good, balanced diet, because her family is active and they need it, even more than most.

When her sons were young, and now again for the sake of little Amy, Mrs. Carter insists on a basic evening meal of meat, vegetables and fruit. She rules out desserts like cakes and cookies— reserving them for treats on special occasions. At lunchtime, the Carter household usually gets salads or sandwiches.

The discovery by Mrs. Carter—after twenty-five years of early breakfasts—that Jimmy Carter didn't like breakfast, and was eating the ones she cooked only to make her happy, came about after the Carters had moved into the governor's mansion in Atlanta.

Telling this story at her own expense in a recent interview, the first lady said, with a deprecating smile, that her husband told her his true feelings about breakfast while they were trying to figure out what hours the mansion help should work.

When they came to the kitchen staff, she noted that at least one person able to prepare a good breakfast should arrive for work about dawn, so the early rising governor could eat before he started the day's schedule.

Jimmy looked her straight in the eye, she relates, and said, firmly: "The best thing about campaigning for governor was that I didn't have to eat breakfast. You made me eat breakfast at home for twenty-five years, and I don't like breakfast!"

Mrs. Carter says that when she entertains visitors at the White House she sticks to the simple foods that her own family likes. And only at formal affairs, for foreign dignitaries and the like, does she bow to protocol and custom and approve the White House kitchen staff's suggestions of more exotic gourmet foods.

Aside from breakfast, which the president now prepares himself if the kitchen staff fails to get in early enough (his breakfast: orange juice and coffee). Mrs. Carter says her husband is easy to please at mealtime. The president has informed her that he has had his fill of steak and roast beef on the campaign trips, so when he is at home he prefers one of his "goulash" dishes, or chicken, fixed in any one of a dozen different ways, with

46

lots of fresh vegetables, or most any kind of seafood you can broil, such as red snapper, shrimp, lobster tails and the like.

Mrs. Carter usually turns thumbs down on sauce mixes, pudding mixes and other convenience foods. Her reason, she says, is that you can never be sure what is put into these mixes and it is her responsibility to know what she serves her family.

The scores of additives the makers are putting into manufactured foods these days trouble her. And now that she is first lady she almost never gets into a grocery store and cannot check the labels. So her defenses are down, in the matter of screening for unsuitable additives. In the White House she almost never does any cooking. Rosalynn Carter thinks the proper authorities should be firm when they suspect that some food or soft drink ingredient is or can be harmful. "They should remove it from the market at once," she says, "and not wait for the long series of tests and investigations. If the tests show that they were wrong, and that it is not harmful, then put it back again, and no harm is done."

Guests invited to the small private dinners at the White House are likely to get grits with their breakfasts. Southern specialties are often served at other meals. The first lady explains that she learned, while Jimmy was governor of Georgia, that visitors from other parts of the country were eager to taste Southern cooking and were invariably disappointed, in a polite way, when she didn't serve a Southern specialty at dinner.

Mrs. Carter's own preferences in food have broadened and become internationalized as a result of their travel during their years in the navy. She has acquired the habit of using a lot of cooking wines and soy sauce for marinades and flavorings, and has a private list of favorite recipes that include Italian, French, Chinese and Indian dishes. But for informal entertaining, her menu has a Southern bias.

A recent German guest, for example, was ecstatic after having a meal of minted fruit cup, quail, tomatoes stuffed with chopped collard greens and sprinkled with bacon, broiled peaches, and peanut butter chiffon pie.

Mrs. Carter hastens to say that is not a dinner she would recommend for a state occasion, only for the more informal affairs.

At home in Plains the Carters keep a stocked liquor cabinet, but serve it only to guests whom they know have indicated a desire for it. The nearest the Carters come to taking intoxicants together is on their anniversaries, when they have a custom of toasting each other in champagne.

When Rosalynn was growing up there were no alcoholic drinks of any kind in the home, and she is even now more comfortable when hard liquor is not involved in her entertaining.

The only use her mother ever had for any alcoholic beverage, she says, was to make the filling for what all of Plains knows as "Miss Allie's Lane Cake," which she makes only at Christmas time.

She confides that her mother's recipe for this special holiday delicacy only calls for half a glass of wine, but that "Miss" Allie had acknowledged, laughingly, to special friends that "it's better with bourbon."

Another whispered secret of the first lady is that she, herself, doesn't eat grits "because they are too fattening."

She reports that the reaction of foreign guests when they are served grits at the White House is as varied as the nationalities of the guests. Brazilian guests just didn't like them, even after they had put sugar on them (which is never done in the South). On the other hand, the Japanese ambassador and his wife had several helpings.

She was asked by one interviewer whether it was her ambition to make the country more conscious of sound nutrition, just as Mrs. Johnson made it her specialty to campaign against highway billboards and for beautification projects generally. Mrs. Carter indicated that she had not made up her mind, but her public statements thus far and her schedule of activities show that she is more immediately interested in making life better and happier for America's senior citizens, and improving the public attitude toward mental illness and upgrading both public and private facilities for treating this disease.

More recently, the first lady has become White House sponsor for a program called "Project Propinquity" which aims at rescuing young victims of the various urban ghettos from a life of failure, by seeing to it that drop-outs and the disadvantaged get the kind of an education they need to become useful citizens.

Projects of this kind—projects that come to grips with the real problems of everyday life—seem to appeal most to First Lady Rosalynn Carter.

Now, here are a few of the favorite recipes collected by Mrs. Carter from family and friends in Plains, Georgia, over the years. First, one from her own mother: "Miss" Allie Smith's famous Lane Cake (for Christmas):

Ingredients: 1 cup butter, 2 cups sugar, 3 cups all-purpose flour, 2 teaspoons baking powder, ¼ teaspoon salt, 1 cup milk, six egg whites (stiffly beaten) and Lane filling (recipe later on).

How to make it: In a bowl, cream butter until smooth. Gradually add sugar and continue beating until mixture is light and smooth. Combine dry ingredients in another bowl and add to creamed mixture alternately with milk. Stir ¼ of beaten egg whites into batter. Fold in remaining egg whites until blended. Spoon batter into 3 greased and floured 9-inch layer cake pans. Bake in a preheated 375 degree oven for 20 to 25 minutes. Cool in pans for 10 minutes then remove and cool on cake racks. Fill and frost top with Lane filling (see below). Cake layers freeze well.

Ingredients for Lane filling: 6 egg yolks, lightly beaten, 1¼ cups sugar, ½ cup butter, 1 cup raisins, 1 cup pecans, chopped; 1 teaspoon vanilla, ¼ cup bourbon or wine.

How to make it: Combine yolks with sugar and butter in a heavy saucepan and cook over medium heat, stirring constantly until sugar dissolves and mixture thickens to coat back of spoon. Do not allow mixture to boil, or eggs will scramble.

Remove from heat and stir in raisins, pecans, vanilla and bourbon or wine. Cool before using to fill and frost cake. Serves 10 to 12. Frosted cake should be allowed to mellow for two to three days before serving.

And now, Rosalynn Carter's own receipe for Strawberry Cake:

Ingredients: 1 package of yellow or white cake mix, 1 3-ounce package strawberry jello, ¾ cup of cooking oil, 1 cup chopped nuts, 4 eggs, 2 tablespoons of flour, 1 10-ounce package of frozen strawberries, or one pint of fresh strawberries with ½ cup sugar.

How to make it: Mix all ingredients and beat well; pour into angel food cake pan and bake at 350 degrees for 45 minutes or until done. Serve plain or with whipped cream.

Here's one from the president's mother, "Miss" Lillian Carter. A recipe for peanut brittle, which she guarantees will make a granddaughter happy:

Ingredients: 3 cups sugar, 1½ cups water, 1 cup white Karo syrup, 3 cups raw peanuts, 2 tablespoons soda, ½ stick butter, 1 teaspoon vanilla.

How to make it: Boil sugar, water and Karo syrup until it spins a thread. Add peanuts. After adding peanuts, stir continually until syrup turns golden brown. Remove from heat and add remaining ingredients. Stir until butter melts. Pour out quickly on 2 cookie sheets with sides. As mixture begins to harden around edges, pull until thin. When it cools, break into pieces.

Here is one of the many dishes the president includes in his "goulash" category. This particular "goulash" is called a "Chicken and Rice Casserole" and it comes from the first lady. It's a presidential favorite.

Ingredients: 1 chicken, cut up and seasoned; ½ stick butter, 1 4-ounce can mushrooms, drained (save liquid); 4 large onions, 2 chicken bouillon cubes, 1 cu. uncooked regular rice (do not use quick cooking rice).

How to make it: Melt butter in casserole. Place chicken in layers with onions and mushrooms. Cook, covered, for 1½ hours at 350 degrees. Remove chicken and add enough boiling water to mushroom liquid to make 4½ cups of broth in casserole. Dissolve bouillon cubes in broth. Add rice, replace chicken and cook for one hour.

Here is another chicken dish from the president's mother. She calls it "Chicken Supreme:"

Ingredients: 4 boned chicken breasts, 1 egg, ¼ cup milk, bread crumbs, oleo, cardamon, chervil, salt and pepper, 2 ounces of brandy, 4 tablespoons Burgundy, 1 pint chicken stock.

How to make it: Season chicken breasts with cardamon, chervil, salt and pepper; dip into egg and milk (beaten together), then dip into fine bread crumbs. Brown on both sides in butter until tender. Place chicken in baking dish and pour the following over chicken: brandy, Burgundy, chicken stock. Bake at 350 degrees until tender.

This recipe of Rosalynn's appeared in the book, *Atlanta Cooks for Company,* which was subsequently designated Atlanta's official cookbook. Rosalynn's contribution, which appears on page 141 was called the "Plains Special Cheese Ring."

Ingredients: 1 pound grated cheddar cheese; 1 cup chopped peanuts; 1 cup mayonnaise; 1 small onion, grated; black pepper to taste; dash of cayenne.

How to make it: Mold all ingredients with hands into desired shape, place in refrigerator and chill. When ready to serve, fill center with strawberry preserves. But it is also good as a cheese spread without preserves.

This one is an example of the more exotic recipes collected by Rosalynn Carter in the course of her navy travels. It's called "Eggplant Porvencale."

Ingredients: 1 large peeled eggplant, cut in 8 one-inch circles; 1 teaspoon salt, ½ teaspoon white pepper, 3 tablespoons butter, 3 tablespoons salad oil, 1 cup chopped onion, 3 cloves minced garlic, 2 cups of peeled, seeded and chopped tomatoes, pinch of thyme, salt and white pepper, ¼ cup chopped parsley, ½ cup white bread crumbs, 1 cup grated Swiss or Gruyere cheese.

How to make it: As the eggplant slices change in circumference, trim so they are all the same size. Place in a shallow, oiled pan. Sprinkle with the salt and pepper. Broil five minutes. In a large fry pan heat the oil and butter. Add onion and garlic. Cook until yellow. Then add tomatoes and trimmings of eggplant. Cook until thick. Stir in seasonings and bread crumbs. Correct seasonings. Pile on the broiled eggplant. Cover with the cheese. Bake at 350 degrees until cheese is melted. (The first lady says this is good cold, also, or as an hors d'oeuvre or salad)

5

The Politician

Every pew was packed at the Gillies Memorial Community Church, in Baltimore, and dozens of standees were being gently pushed back along the walls where they would not block the aisles. The congregation, 99.9 percent black, was at capacity every Sunday in that church. The pastor, the Rev. Theodore Jackson was a colorful figure and a popular preacher, a favorite of the black community. But on this Sunday in April the sanctuary's capacity clearly was being severely tested. Word had spread that Mrs. Jimmy Carter, wife of the presidential candidate whom many of the city's blacks were reportedly supporting, was coming to church that morning. And there were rumors she might even talk to them. But the usual closing time already had been passed, and the preacher had called on a singer, and the singer had been followed by the church clerk who was reading off announcement after announcement in an obvious effort to keep the crowd happy and seated.

A pair of ushers with carnations in their lapels stood on the front sidewalk waving away a line of automobiles from a reserved parking space below the steps. The curb along Park Heights Avenue was parked solid for blocks.

The clock ticked on, with announcements and songs and then more announcements. There was a murmur of whispering, but nobody left the pews. Finally, nearly forty-five minutes beyond the usual benediction time, the doors in the rear of the sanctuary opened, and there was a general rustling as hundreds of close-packed bodies twisted to watch two white ladies make their way down the side aisle past a double row of standees to a reserved space on the front pew near the altar. A young white man, walking behind them, paused halfway down and took up a stand along the wall.

The announcements continued for another two or three minutes, partly inaudible because of a rising mumble of conversation.

"Is that her? Is that Mrs. Carter? Yes. Which one? She looks young. Are you sure that's her?"

Then the pastor rose and walked to the pulpit.

"Well, our special guest is here now, and I'm sure you all know who she is and you have seen her

on television," he said. "And now you are going to
get to see her in person because she's kindly
consented to bring us a message from her
husband. And her husband, as many of you know,
is a real Christian gentleman who many of us hope
the Lord is going to give us as our next great
president.

"Yes! Yes! Amen! Praise the Lord!" the people
responded.

"So here is Mrs. Carter now. Will you please
come up here, Mrs. Carter, where we can all see
you and hear you?"

Looking slim and pretty in a simple beige cotton
dress with a high neckline, and wearing no
noticeable make-up, Rosalynn Carter seemed a
little confused over the way to the steps to the
platform, and walked uncertainly across the front
of the sanctuary.

From the rear pew where the ushers had seated
this lone white man, by asking two young blacks to
stand, Rosalynn looked like a shy young girl about
to make a speech at commencement exercises, and
terrified at the thought of facing the crowd. But it
soon became clear that she knew what she was
doing.

Already that Sunday morning she had talked to
two other black congregations—the first at eleven
o'clock, and she was fresh from a tour that
brought her before audiences in every state,
literally hundreds of them. But the look of

semi-frightened shyness stuck with her, and for this audience, at least, it was an asset.

Before she uttered her first words, they responded with warm-hearted sympathy.

"Help her, Lord! Isn't she nice? Help her, help her." As she began to speak they leaned forward, eagerly.

"It is pleasant to be here this morning and to join you in praising the Lord, and to have the opportunity to say a few words about my husband, Jimmy Carter, who is running for president," she began in soft Georgian tones.

"Amen, Amen."

"In his inaugural address as governor of Georgia, he said: 'The time for racial discrimination is over. No longer shall any poor, weak or black person be deprived of the opportunity of an education, a job or simple justice.' "

It was a speech that in substance, had been delivered over and over many times before, but it seemed fresh and new to these people, and she did have the knack of delivering it as if from the heart, and as if it was something she had just thought of at that moment.

The responses rose to a higher level.

"He felt a responsibility for those people in our state who are affected by government," she continued. "He lived up to this responsibility. You know, if you are wealthy, you don't need so many of these services. The wealthy can send their children to private schools. They don't have to worry about the welfare department."

"Yes, yes! That's right! Amen, sister!"

"I wish I had the time to tell you of all the things he did," she went on, speaking softly and earnestly. "We had one of the worst systems of government in this nation in Georgia. But at the end of four years with Jimmy Carter in the state house, we had one of the best systems of government. I, myself, worked with the health department of our state. We had one of the worst. Now we have one of the best. That is why I say it was a gratifying experience for me.

"We looked around, and there were no portraits in the Capitol of our great black leaders. So we put up the portraits of Martin Luther King, Jr. and others."

The "amens" and "hallelujahs" reached a new crescendo.

"My husband deputized all the high school principals as voter registrars, to see that every high school student was registered to vote before he reached the age of eighteen. Dr. Martin Luther King, Sr. is my good friend," she declared, emphasizing the word "friend."

The audience nodded, knowingly, look at each other, and there was an undertone of approving comments.

"The day his wife was shot in his church, Jimmy

was in a Democratic telethon in California, so I went to Mr. King's house to be with him through that time.

"I was in his church the last Sunday he preached in his own church. He'll never stop preaching. And Dr. King told me that day that he thought my husband would be a great president and that he was with him all the way. . . .

There was a swelling chorus of approval.

"Another thing I want you to know about my husband," she went on, "is that he's a Christian man. He has told me many times that he spent more time on his knees as governor of Georgia, than in all the rest of his life put together."

"Yes, yes! Praise the Lord. Thank you, God!"

"We need your help," she said, "so that with your help and the help of our Lord Jesus Christ, Jimmy Carter can be a great president of these United States."

As the petite Southern lady left the pulpit and made her way back to the pew, where she stood as the pastor pronounced the long-delayed benediction, it occurred to this lone white man, standing in the back row, near the door, that that was one of the most effective, most undebatable, unanswerable political speeches he had heard in his half-century career of listening to and writing about politicians. Jimmy Carter, he was sure, would get all the votes in this crowd without bothering to say a word on his own behalf.

Rosalynn had said just enough, and no more.

Throughout the campaign, it was Rosalynn who concentrated on wooing the blacks. The psychology was good. As the election finally turned out, her presence in the black ghettos, without bodyguard and usually with only one other white woman and a driver, was a living refutation of the myth that Southern white ladies don't dare venture into black neighborhoods.

She ate at black restaurants and slept in black-run hotels and ignored the insulting remarks of rednecks on the fringes of her campaign crowds, who hooted "nigger-lover," and worse, from safe distance.

It was in a Southern black restaurant, where I managed to slip into a seat at her table, that I heard her clearest explanation of the way she regarded the relationship between the will of the Lord and the Carter campaign.

She told me she was certain that it was God's will that Jimmy run for president, but did not go so far as to presume that it was God's will for him to win.

"We both pray constantly that he will not permit us to overstep his will," she said. "We are pleased the way things are going and we think we are doing it the way God wants us to do it. We are talking about positive things. We are not attacking other people who are running, because one of those others might even yet be God's choice for the presidency."

I remarked at one point that the most surprising thing about the Carter successes was that the people running his campaign were "just kids," and inexperienced kids, at that.

"Do you think that might be some sort of a sign, that he's winning in spite of this assortment of amateurs and novices?" I asked. "Do you think this might be a sign that somebody up there is really in charge, and that all these kids are doing is just 'fronting' for the Lord?"

Mrs. Carter stiffened and bristled slightly at these demeaning remarks about her campaign workers, about ninty percent of them really just a gathering of happy youngsters.

"Most of our staff people," she said with an edge in her voice, "though they are young, have been with Jimmy since he won the governorship. Now that is six whole years of political experience, so who are your novices and your amateurs?"

And she went on: "I don't know about signs. But I know we do pray daily for guidance, not for signs. And I am sure we are doing what God wants us to do."

"But what about your happy young 'experienced' staff workers?" I asked. "I've heard them talking with reporters, and among themselves. And the language some of them use occasionally doesn't sound like it's coming from Christians."

"Don't you ever find that because these youngsters may not be thinking or acting on the same wavelength as you or your husband—and may or may not be committed to the Lord's service—that there are frequent misunderstandings, disagreements or difficulties?"

"Oh, I don't really know," she said. "Maybe sometimes we have differences about what to say and how to say it and how to run the campaign. But remember, it's Jimmy's campaign and the final decisions are his. Jimmy is his own campaign manager, no matter who has the title. The positions Jimmy takes are his own. So what does it matter if the staff disagrees?"

I got in one more question on Carter's views of religion and the presidency before his fast-moving wife finished her meal and took off for the next campaign stop.

"What makes your husband think that a dedicated Christian can be a successful president when this country is full of people who don't believe—like the Jews and people of other religions—plus all the millions who are just nominal Christians, and who look on a strong Christian as a fanatic?"

"My husband believes," she said, speaking slowly and choosing her words carefully, "that if he turns to God in prayer before he makes a decision, that he will make the right decison. He is especially prayerful before making decisions that might affect the lives of people.

"He was a good governor, and as a governor he used the same approach; he always asked for God's guidance. And he found no conflict between his religious faith and what he had to do as head of the state government. I think the same thing will be true when he is president. And there are so many more ways to serve the Lord and to serve the people as president than there were as governor."

"Why," I asked quickly as she rose to go, "did Jimmy have so much trouble with Lester Maddox, who also professes a strong faith in God, and who prays a lot?" I recalled that it was Maddox who insisted on prayer sessions in the legislature, a custom which was discontinued under Carter's governorship.

"Christians," she replied, "have as many opinions as non-Christians. They are free to agree with each other, or disagree. Maddox chose to disagree."

It was the end of a typical seventeen-hour day for the campaigning wife of candidate Jimmy Carter. He had just squeezed out another primary campaign victory by a narrow margin in Michigan. Rosalynn and a carload of weary staffers were headed for the hotel and for bed.

Most of them were dozing. But Rosalynn was still checking to see that everything was being done right, with her eye on the fall campaign she was certain they would be engaged in soon.

"Be sure to make a list of all the supporters we've spent a night with while we campaigned here," she said. "I want each one of them to come and spend a night in the White House, and I must not leave anyone out."

To Rosalynn Carter, veteran of three political wars—two for the governorship and one for the presidency—details like this are what make the difference between a winner and a loser.

For most of the spring primary season, and then again through the fall general election drive, Rosalynn was on her own. Her husband usually was hundreds or thousands of miles away.

It was a sort of "you take the East Coast and I'll take the West Coast and we'll divide what's in the middle" mom and pop effort. And the campaigning was just as real, just as "substantive" for Rosalynn as it was for Jimmy. They conferred daily by phone. And it soon became apparent to reporters and other questioners that they could get Jimmy's answers just as easily and just as accurately and in as much detail by asking Rosalynn as they could by asking Jimmy. And Rosalynn also seemed easier to approach than her husband. And, in addition, she almost always gave more time to the questioners.

For Rosalynn, then forty-eight, the campaign was a seventeen-to-eighteen-hour round of thousands of handshakes, thousands of speeches, pleasant answers to rather "dumb" questions, being nice when you felt like screaming with fatigue, getting up every morning knowing that this would be another day of the same, and learning to smile at yourself in the mirror and tell yourself it was all worthwhile.

The Carter team—and the fact that they do work as a team became apparent very early, so it should be no surprise they are working as a team now that they are in the White House—is highly unusual in that their impulses seem always to be on the same wavelength.

Rosalynn says she has had disagreements with Jimmy, but she never can specify offhand what they were—except for the one big one, when Jimmy decided to quit the navy and go back home, and Rosalynn balked because she was seeing the world for the first time and loved it. But, as it turned out, "Jimmy was right," she acknowledges.

They both have that deceptively soft Southern drawl, capped by a sweet smile that masks a steely self-discipline, absolute self-assurance, firmly-set and specific ambitions, a toughness in the face of difficulty and a stubbornness that refuses to admit defeat.

"No one has ever told me what to do or say," Rosalynn said once, commenting on her style of campaigning. "I do and I say what I think is right, and if I have prayed about it first, I can be sure it *will* be right."

Even her mother-in-law, "Miss" Lillian Carter, gives her high marks as an efficient partner in her son's political life.

"She's very ambitious," the elder Mrs. Carter comments. "And Rosalynn will be a force to be reckoned with in the White House, you'll see. She has more influence on Jimmy than anyone else. Even if I, his mother, want Jimmy to do something, I ask Rosalynn first. She can do anything in the world with Jimmy. He listens to her. He thinks she has a great mind."

Campaign manager Hamilton Jordan echoed this story, during the fall election.

"If Jody Powell and I strike out, the best thing to do is get Rosalynn on our side," he said. But he added that he uses this tactic as sparingly as possible because he doesn't want to "use up all my leverage."

Rosalynn Carter has that rare ability to make every campaign speech sound as if it is extemporaneous and that she just thought of it and is giving whatever crowd she is speaking to, fresh material for the first time.

She extols her husband at each stop with a sincerity and fervor that gives no hint she has said those same words over and over hundreds of times.

"Our whole life has been a challenge," Rosalynn tells reporters who ask why this small-town couple took on themselves the job of conquering the world.

But reporters who have followed Mrs. Carter's campaign, and Jimmy's, agree that in spite of their last six years of constantly public life, they still remain very private people.

No matter how well you know them, say their friends, you never shake the feeling that Rosalynn and Jimmy are members of a two-person private club that is so exclusive that even their own children are only honorary members, with strictly limited privileges to the secret life of the two full members.

Rosalynn got good laughs all across the country when she said that she and Jimmy are well trained to live in the White House—which is so constantly in the spotlight that it is frequently likened to a goldfish bowl.

"We're used to that kind of life," she explains. "We grew up and still live in a town with a population of 683.

"Everybody in town knows everything I've ever done. And the same goes for Jimmy. And there's never been a hint of scandal in Jimmy's public or private life."

Carter's mother, however, casts a little doubt on Rosalynn's insistence that all of Plains knows everything about her. "I admire her, of course," says "Miss" Lillian. "But I have never seen her let her hair down. I've never heard her tell a joke." But that's all the mother-in-law will tell you. "I never talk about my daughter-in-law," she says. And that ends the conversation.

Rosalynn's style of person-to-person campaigning is effective and exceedingly personal. She will walk through a crowd, touching people as she goes. Now and then she will take a stranger by the hand and lean close and whisper something into his or her ear, that gives everybody around the impression she has confided something. It gives the person she has whispered to a special lift—a feeling that he was picked out of the crowd for personal notice. His friends ask him about her. The more they ask, the more expert and complimentary he becomes on the subject of Rosalynn and Jimmy Carter. After all, everybody saw her whisper to him.

Usually, all she has whispered is something like: "Vote for my husband." But nobody knows this except Rosalynn and the person she whispered to, and he or she is not going to admit it because it's too much fun acting like he's a personal friend who knows all the campaign secrets.

After Rosalynn had passed through a crowd and done her usual amount of whispering into local ears, the Carter campaign in that area almost always picked up steam. It's a trick that worked over and over, the same way.

Like the politician she is, Rosalynn has no trouble shifting gears when the occasion demands it.

On one occasion she was scheduled to make a speech at a red-white-and-blue flag-waving bicentennial affair somewhere out in the West. There was to be singing by a four hundred voice choir which had a repertoire of religious songs, and someone on the local Carter committee suggested that she might insert some religious comments in her speech to keep it in line with the spirit of the music.

So, after the choir had rendered its version of the song "I am Thankful to be an American," it was Rosalynn's turn to speak.

She told them first what a great experience it was to be there on that occasion and listen to that beautiful music that simultaneously praised our country and praised the Lord.

Then, after describing her candidate husband as a hard-working farmer and an honest governor, she added that he is "deeply religious."

"We both grew up in Christian homes. The church is the center of life in Plains. Jimmy has said many times that he spent more time on his knees as governor of Georgia than in all the rest of his life. We need your help. We need your prayers."

The audience roared its approval. Rosalynn had correctly sensed the mood of one more campaign audience and scored again for her husband.

Rosalynn has never shied away from hard work. Without any help in her home she worked full-time at the peanut warehouse keeping books and doing all the other office chores, from the time they returned to Plains from the navy. All the while she was raising her three sons. Her son Chip, when asked to describe his mother, scratched his head and said, "She is active."

After the hard life she had as a child, and the tough years getting the family business on a paying basis, why, she has been asked over and over, did she take on this vastly harder life as political campaigner and as an active working first lady.

"I think," she replies, "that as first lady I can help change things."

And then she adds: "I'm not doing all this just for Jimmy. I feel I'm doing it for the country."

She knows that public figures get about an equal amount of criticism and praise, and she's braced and ready for it.

"We've had some bitter times, right in Plains when we were running the business. We were boycotted several times because of our stand that blacks should have the same rights to attend our church as whites. And we were boycotted because we led the effort to consolidate the black and white schools.

ROSALYNN

"But all that is behind us. And it taught us that if
you stand up for what you think is right, people
will, in the end, come to respect you, and you will
come out the winner. I think, after all our battles,
Jimmy's election to the presidency proves to us
and to the world that you don't have to
compromise with God's law to get ahead, even in
this sinful world."

6

The Daughter

"I am Amy Carter," she wrote in painfully neat script on a page of the reporter's notebook, her mouth slightly twisted in concentration, and the tip of her tongue showing at one corner of it. "I will be ten years old in October," she volunteered verbally, "and on my achievement test it said that I could read as well as a thirteen-years-old-and-four-months person." And then she added, as an afterthought, as she skipped away: "Anyone who doesn't like to read is dumb."

"That," commented a neighbor from Plains, "is Amy Carter at her Amy Carterest."

Amy, still only a few feet away, turned and asked: "What did you say?"

"I was just wondering what you wanted for a

birthday present," the neighbor lied.

"What I'd like most for a present," she said, "is a walkie-talkie like the ones the secret service guys carry around. And I think I'm going to get one."

Amy, a strawberry blonde, with freckles, and what she herself tells newsmen are "robin's-egg blue" eyes, is described by her teachers as "very verbal" which is a teacher's way of saying she talks a lot. She also giggles a lot. She has always turned in straight-A averages on her school report card, and, according to various members of her family, "she really doesn't seem to have to study very hard."

She herself modestly claims that she can "sew, cook, play the piano, and roller skate." And she adds that she can also "hang for ten minutes" from a tree upside down.

Unpredictable Amy allowed that the White House was a great place to live. She came to this conclusion after inspecting the place and finding that it had a bowling alley, a billiard table, a swimming pool, and best of all, a private little movie theater where she occasionally brings her friends to see a Disney movie.

But she was lukewarm about the long political campaign the family had to go through to pay the rent on that place.

"Campaigning might not be so bad," she commented, "if you didn't have to wear a dress." Now that the campaign is over and she has settled down in her new home, Amy says she is going back to the "no-dress" rule that held in Plains.

When her father first told her he was going to run for president, she thought it exciting "because he might win." But then, on thinking it over a little more carefully, she decided she didn't want him to run, or at least, she didn't want him to win. And why? Because she had to move from Plains to Atlanta when he was elected governor of Georgia, and that cured her of all desire to live in a big city, and she was sure Washington was the same kind of place.

"I was glad when we came back to Plains," Amy recalls now, "because Plains is just about the right size. I can go to school, or anyplace, on my bike. And all my friends live in Plains."

Amy is a stickler for precise accuracy, like her father. When you talk to her and you take notes, she always insists on reading over your shoulder what you are writing down, to make sure you get it right.

In the midst of a sober discussion of her grades at school or her father's job as president, Amy is the kind who is likely to volunteer something like: "I can stand on my head. Do you want to see me do it? I can do somersaults, too." Quite often she demonstrates without waiting for an answer.

Her paternal grandmother, "Miss" Lillian Carter admits that she spoils the child shamefully, when she baby-sits, which is something she seldom gets to do now that Rosalynn and Jimmy have moved to Washington. The elder Mrs. Carter sticks to her isolated "pond house" a mile and a half out of Plains. But she shrugged helplessly when she admitted it, when I interviewed her on a warm summer afternoon in her parlor, overlooking the pond where bass were leaping after flies.

"She has a mind of her own," the grandmother commented, "and she wouldn't be a Carter if she didn't have. She didn't like all that campaigning, but she usually did her part when they asked her to."

"Her part" included a sort of clog dance before the cameras of the Grand Ole Opry, and struggling into a hated lacy dress a number of times for "just one more" picture by the photographers.

"Do you enjoy going to church and Sunday school?" a reporter asked.

"I like Sunday school best," she volunteered, "because you don't have to sit still so long, and you can talk when they start asking questions."

"Are you a real Christian?"

She indicated that she felt she was. Amy was baptized at the First Baptist Church in Washington, D.C. on Sunday, February 6, 1977 after being questioned privately about her faith by the pastor, the Rev. Dr. Charles A. Trentham, and after making a public confession of faith in Jesus

Christ before the congregation of more than a thousand, including her parents, and her beloved governess, Mrs. Mary Fitzpatrick.

Apparently thinking over the question about her Christian faith, Amy volunteered: "I had a dream about God. He was an old man with a brown beard."

"Brown?"

"Yes, brown, not white."

The president says it was Amy who, after her own baptism, had a serious talk with Mrs. Fitzpatrick. As a result, the governess made up her mind to join the church and be baptized herself.

The thirty-one-year-old black lady was released early from a Georgia prison where she was serving a sentence for murder, so she could come to Washington and be with Amy. She has been with the president's daughter since Carter moved into the governor's mansion in 1970, and there is almost a mother-daughter kind of affection between her and the child.

It was Amy who was the first to run and hug Mrs. Fitzpatrick when she was voted into membership in the fashionable First Baptist Church without a single hand raised in opposition, late in March, 1977. Later, when she was baptized, it was Amy who held her tightly by the arm as the two of them walked back toward the church door after the benediction, a broad smile spreading across both of their faces.

The president and Rosalynn take baptism seriously, especially the baptism of their young daughter. It is the custom in the Southern Baptist church that no one is baptized until he or she is old enough to know what baptism means, and old enough to decide himself if he thinks he is ready for it.

So when the time came for Amy to be baptized, Dr. Trentham gave the president and his wife a copy of his book, *Daring Discipleship*, for Amy to study in preparation for the event. Rosalynn reported that her daughter read the book through, and then said she thought she would like to go ahead and become a Christian and a member of the church.

The first lady admitted that she has seen in the press some questions about the timing of her daughter's baptism. "Was it necessary to wait until the family moved to Washington? Was it done then deliberately, for propaganda purposes or maybe for political reasons?"

That kind of talk irritates Rosalynn and she ignores it. Her friends say that she knows the whole country realizes the Carters are Christians of long standing, and that they don't need any newspaper publicity to prove it. But that kind of talk is a part of politics that gets under her skin.

Rosalynn doesn't think her only daughter has been much affected by the attention she is getting.

"She's very well adjusted, and I'm proud of her," the first lady told reporters. "She was only three when Jimmy was elected governor of Georgia, and she soon got used to crowds and having people pay her a lot of attention. And she's been in the middle of the same political things ever since, for almost seven years. Now she doesn't pay any attention to all the publicity she's getting.

"She doesn't read the newspapers, she doesn't watch the news and she ignores the reporters," she added, smiling at the newsmen around her.

People have criticized the Carters for taking Amy along to state dinners, and seeing the child's picture in the next morning's papers, sleepily slumped in a chair between her parents, wearing a long, lacy robe and reading a book.

"Amy attends some state dinners because we like her to be with us," Rosalynn explains simply. "She reads books on those occasions because she's fidgety and can't sit still. If you were going to that kind of a party, wouldn't you like to take a book?" The first lady smiled.

Rosalynn doesn't give her daughter an allowance any more. She used to get one when they lived in Plains, but the opportunity for spending is limited behind the cast iron fence surrounding the White House. And when Amy goes outside the fence she is always accompanied by an adult, a secret service agent or another member of the family, so money is available if the occasion arises or if Amy can work up a good case for demanding some.

The young Carter daughter has spent much of her life around adults and her conversation tends to show it. That was one reason why the Carters decided on a public school in Washington, rather than having her schooled by a tutor in the White House, as the Kennedys did their daughter Caroline.

They chose the Thaddeus Stevens school, about six blocks from the White House, for several reasons. First, because it was close, and second, because it was a progressive school, one of the showplaces of the District of Columbia school system.

The school's population is almost a cross section of the world population. Located near a number of foreign embassies, the students' nationalities are widely scattered and their skins are all shades.

Overall, as in most other schools in the capital, the students are sixty per cent blacks. In Plains, Amy's school was also black by about the same percentage.

Amy's special friend, whom she brings home to the White House on occasions to view a movie with her is Claudia Sanchez, the daughter of a Chilean embassy cook.

There are 215 pupils in the 108-year-old brick school building, the oldest still operating in the city of Washington. Its eleven classrooms cover a range from pre-kindergarten to the sixth grade. Amy's class combines the fourth and fifth grades, because there are only seven full-time teachers. But the staff is backed by twenty-five teachers' assistants and a librarian. And the school is also equipped with an MIT computer specially designed to increase mathematical and reading skills.

It's a cheery place, despite its age. The Stevens school was named for a northern abolitionist when it was built in 1869, and the neighborhood then was considered an elegant location. Now it is surrounded by office buildings.

The inside of the school was completely refurnished only ten years ago. Its classrooms are carpeted, and the classroom walls are painted in blue-green and salmon. The windows are large and the rooms are well-lighted.

In Amy's class they studied reading, spelling, math, social sciences, science, music and art. And Amy also had her choice of taking sessions of ballet, gymnastics, photography, sewing, cooking and carpentry.

Amy chose to stay late three nights a week for Spanish lessons, explaining that her mother and father are taking Spanish, too, and she wanted to surprise them.

There is a semi-secret reason why the Carters chose this school for Amy, and it has nothing to do with the school's proximity to the White House or the progressive nature of the teaching.

Rosalynn has confided to her assistants that she was sold on the school immediately when she met Amy's prospective teacher—Verona Meeder, forty-five, the wife of a Methodist pastor, the mother of three dedicated Christian childen and an enthusiastic evangelical herself.

I talked to Mrs. Meeder after Amy had joined her class. And it soon became apparent why the wife of the president was so taken with her. Her childhood and her Christian background parallel Rosalynn's almost exactly. And more than that, Mrs. Meeder showed all the signs of being a teacher who teaches because she loves the work and loves children. Even more, the Carters were impressed that all three of the Meeder children are active in the Campus Crusade For Christ in their respective schools.

Verona Meeder told me that she was brought up on a farm near the tiny hamlet of Deep Run, North Carolina, and her family still lives there. The first lady, who came from the same environment, felt that this good lady would certainly understand the fears and questions of a little girl suddenly transplanted from Plains, Georgia, to the White House.

The teacher's husband is the Rev. Andrew K. Meeder, pastor of the Lanham, Maryland First Methodist Church. She told me that she was brought up a Methodist, but joined the Baptist

Church because most of her childhood friends were Baptists. Now—married to a Methodist pastor—she's back where her family started her. That, too, is parallel with Rosalynn's personal history. The wife of the president was brought up a Methodist, and became a Baptist only after she married.

As if she doesn't get enough teaching in the course of the school year, Amy's teacher takes over the teaching of a Bible school class in the summer. And throughout the year she is a substitute teacher in the Sunday school, and active in the United Methodist Women.

After Mrs. Carter's first visit to the school—a visit unaccompanied by Amy—Mrs. Meeder suggested to her class that they all write letters to Amy, addressed to her home in Plains, so she would feel that she was going to be among friends when she came to Washington.

Mrs. Meeder also wrote, and among other things she told the president's daughter that the Meeder family dog, a female springer spaniel, had just given birth to a litter of puppies. She sent along a newspaper clipping showing herself with the puppies, and asked if Amy would like to have one.

So, on December 20, 1976, a letter from Plains arrived at the Meeder home in Lanham. Addressed in childish, but easily legible handwriting, it read:

"Dear Mrs. Meeder: Thank you for writing to me. I am looking forward to being in your class. I would like to have a puppy. I think they are cute. My mother is coming to Washington before Christmas. I hope I can come with her, Love, Amy. P.S. Tell the class thanks for the letters."

Thus it was that President Carter, burdened with the job of choosing his Cabinet officers, was relieved by his small daughter of the task of choosing the next official White House dog.

When Amy saw the black and white pup, with its sad, appealing eyes, it was a case of instant and mutual love. His name is now "Grits," in honor of his mistress' Georgia upbringing, and he has joined Amy's cat, which bears the mysterious name of "Misty Malarky Ying Yang" as a permanent resident of the White House—for at least four years, anyway.

"She really loves that dog," says the official keeper of the kennel.

Now that the Carter family has settled down to the routine of the White House, a new house rule has been posted in the press room: "There will be no more interviews with Amy."

The decision was Rosalynn's. She said that she felt it best, for a time, to shield her daughter against excess exposure. So Amy has all but disappeared from the Washington papers. But West Wing White House reporters hear that Amy is still doing well for herself. They hear she has carved out a separate domain in the residential floor.

She has taken over as her private enclave the girlish pink bedroom that once was Tricia Nixon's. Her treasured doll house is in the hallway, and her other possessions scattered and draped on shelves and on the dresser and in the closets.

It is related by one of the presidential press staff that about three o'clock one afternoon toward the end of the school year, in the midst of a conference with his senior aides, President Carter rose from his chair, looked anxiously at his wrist watch and announced:

"There's only one thing more important than this. I've got to go see Amy's teacher." And he walked out.

It was in the happy days immediately after the election of President Carter—a time when Amy was selling lemonade in Plains at outrageous prices, renting her bike to reporters at equally steep fees—a money-making spree that was finally halted by her mother for fear, it is said, that her small daughter might get the wrong idea about the advantages of the free enterprise economic system; it was at about this time that Amy was challenged at one of her press briefings to prove what she was saying.

What she was saying was that she, at the age of just over nine years, was a "real good cook."

So somebody in the group surrounding her—it was probably a reporter—challenged her to prove it. She was stumped for a moment, but then you could see from the gleam in her "robin's-egg-blue" eyes that she had risen to the occasion.

"You can't come into my yeard where I could cook, because the secret service won't let you," she said. "But I've got a good idea. I'll just give ya'll one of my favorite recipes."

So, published here is the favorite recipe of Cook Amy Carter, then nine years old, of Plains, Georgia:

She calls the dish "Puffy Mallow Snowballs."

To make it requires a toaster, a cookie sheet, an ice cream scoop, a pancake turner and two dessert plates, her directions say.

The ingredients: 2 frozen waffles (4½ inches across), ⅔ cup of chocolate ice cream, 1 cup of miniature marshmallows and 2 tablespoons of chocolate flavored topping.

And this is the way she said to make it:

1. Toast two waffles, then cool for about 15 minutes. Place them on ungreased cookie sheet.
2. Place one scoop of ice cream in the center of each waffle.
3. Quickly place the waffles in freezer. Freeze for about one hour, or until the ice cream is firm.
4. About ten minutes before serving, heat oven to 500 degrees.

5. Just before serving, take one waffle out of the freezer and press ½ cup of the marshmallows into the ice cream. Return the first waffle to the cookie sheet in the freezer. Take the second waffle out of the freezer and press the remaining ½ cup of marshmallows into the ice cream. Then return the second waffle to the cookie sheet in the freezer.

6. When ready to serve bake in 500 degree oven for three minutes, or until the marshmallows are light brown. Watch it closely, so you can take them out as soon as they are ready.

7. Lift the two waffles to two dessert plates with pancake turner. Drizzle one tablespoon of chocolate-flavored syrup over each dessert. Then serve, right away quick, before the ice cream melts.

Note: The marshmallows and waffles keep the ice cream from melting in the oven. It would be better if you could make more than two at a time, but I guess you can't. Signed: Amy Carter

7

The Team

Before Jimmy Carter had been in office three months the word began to spread that something new was afoot in the White House.

For the first time, it was whispered, a president and his wife both were operating on the highest government level, almost as a team.

Rosalynn Carter, it was said, was sitting in secret foreign policy sessions, was being consulted in the Oval Office on both national and world issues, and was virtually a Cabinet member without portfolio.

Then, in the late spring of 1977, it all became open and official. The first lady, it was announced, would tour Latin America for two weeks to talk with heads of state, as the president's roving ambassador.

The country watched the news and waited, and

wondered if this quiet lady could pull it off. Would the Latin leaders be insulted that the president had sent a woman, even though she was his wife, to talk to them of substantive issues at the summit level?

But the word had gone ahead of her, that Rosalynn was the one person always closest to the president's ear. So they greeted her in every country like a presidential ambassador should be greeted. She told them of the new administration's plans and policies, and they told her frankly what they thought and planned. And everywhere she went, she left a trail of goodwill.

The trip was a triumph.

The United States Senate made it official by sending the first lady a unanimous message of congratulations when she returned, a message from senators of both parties.

And they underlined it by congratulating the president for having the good sense to send her.

Then the people of the country began to get the message. A national public opinion poll reported that seventy-four percent of Americans had decided that Mrs. Carter was capable and "had handled herself well as a goodwill ambassador for the United States."

In the same nationwide poll, seventy-two percent said they felt it better that information on problems with other countries be given to the president's wife than to the State Department, because she would be sure to get it to the president, while it might get distorted or lost on the way to the White House from the State Department.

And sixty-eight percent of the people approved of the way Rosalynn Carter was handling the role of first lady.

The sweet sound of these endorsements was made even sweeter by the fact that the Carters had not yet been in office a full six months.

While the president was still enjoying the glow of these happy reports, he impulsively granted an exclusive, individual interview to a talented lady reporter for *Newsweek* magazine, Eleanor Clift.

What he told her provided a most intimate picture of the relationship between the chief executive and his wife of thirty-one years.

"I don't know how other husbands and wives are—I can only think the best—but we have an absolutely unconstrained relationship, an ability to express our doubts and concerns to each other. . . . There's very seldom a decision that I make that I don't first discuss with her—either to tell her after the fact what I have done, or, very frequently, to tell her my options and seek her advice," he said.

"She's got superb political judgment. She probably knows the human aspect of the American people and their relationship to the government better than me. . . .

"And she's approachable. She's still approachable. When former old friends of mine come into the Oval Office, they're nervous and tense, and sometimes inarticulate. But they can talk to Rosalynn. Sometimes they even came to see me about a problem and they couldn't broach it. So they call Rosalynn and say, 'This is what I want to tell Jimmy.' Since I am in this position, she's even more attuned [than I] to what the average American wants.

"She doesn't dominate me and doesn't try to. And vice versa. But when we have a serious concern in either direction, we really stop and consider our attitudes.

"When different members of my staff try unsuccessfully to get to me to change my mind about something, they'll go to Rosalynn. And when Rosalynn comes to me and says: 'I need to talk to you about something very seriously—Ham [Jordan] or Jody [Powell] or Stu Eizenstat or Charlie Kirbo have come to me,' I consider that to be the ultimate approach to my consciousness.

"We used the word 'substantive' [about her trip] with trepidation. The trepidation was on her part, because she felt the leaders of those countries would expect too much of her.

"I didn't feel any trepidation. I felt they would underestimate Rosalynn.

"I know what she knows, and her analytical ability, and her capability of evoking accurately

92

what her nation stands for. She's always surprised people. When we go out of the White House she will have left behind a good legacy of quiet achievement."

Before the reporter left, the president, realizing what an all-inclusive endorsement he had given the first lady, smilingly told her that he felt he should add this one thing: "I make the strategic decisions and the major decisions."

By her own wit and grit and proximity Rosalynn has thus become a real part of the Carter presidency.

Her input, according to White House insiders, is more political than policy-forming. She is less isolated and insulated in the White House than is the president, and so she serves him, in the words of her son, Jack, "almost like another Cabinet member on generally what people are thinking and saying." But she is also a valued counselor.

It was Rosalynn who urged Carter to enter *all* the primaries in his long-shot bid for the presidency. And it turned out to be an important part of the winning strategy.

It was Rosalynn who kept reminding him during the fall election that he won in the primaries because he promised to stop wasting money and stop spending money the government had to borrow. She repeated this reminder every time he started talking about some massive new social program.

It was Rosalynn, friends say, who got Carter back on the winning track after he lost the first of the debates with Ford. "Tell it like you were talking to me, forget all those statistics," she is quoted as saying.

It is Rosalynn who is the original fiscal conservative in the family—the girl born on the wrong side of the tracks who helped her mother support the family. She always kept the books for the family firm, and Jimmy never knew how they were doing until she told him. It was she who wrote the checks and balanced the family checkbook.

It was Rosalynn who argued that he should stick to his aim to balance the budget by 1981, no matter how hopeless the project might look.

It has always been Rosalynn who was the only person who dared stand up to Carter and tell him he was wrong, no matter how many others were telling him he was right. She feels strongly about the amount of good the Carters can do as a team. In addition, she would feel she had committed a sin if she did not use her influence as first lady to the utmost every day of her time in that high office.

They work together so closely that many of their friends say they really don't know who influences whom the most—whether Rosalynn is a carbon copy of Jimmy, or Jimmy a carbon copy of Rosalynn. Their personalities seem to have merged. In more than thirty years of marriage they have grown together, instead of growing apart.

A good illustration of the first lady's role in the White House hierarchy, according to an aide, was provided during the days when the papers were full of rumors and speculation that the president had decided to retain Arthur Burns in his job as Chairman of the Federal Reserve Board.

Several aides tried to find out if the newspaper rumors were true.

Finally, they report, the President, in exasperation declared: "I haven't talked yet to Bert [Lance], or to Charlie [Schultze] or to Mike [Blumenthal]! I haven't even talked to Rosalynn!"

The inference of that little word "even," of course, was that Rosalynn was the first on the list to be consulted on who would be the best man to head the Federal Reserve system.

Although she does not try to dominate him or to push him, the president had inadvertently often made it clear that he does feel dependent upon her.

While she was out of the country for two weeks on the Latin tour, he said he guessed he hadn't signed ten checks in ten years. The handling of the family budget is entirely in the hands of Mrs. Carter, who learned to be frugal and thrifty as the daughter of a mother who was widowed at thirty-four and who so successfully managed her personal affairs that she was able to finance college educations for all four of her children.

He listens to his wife, anytime she speaks. Just before she left for Latin America, the president held a press briefing and was answering questions at such great length that the conference was running well past the expected time.

As he talked on, Mrs. Carter, who was present, grew noticeably impatient, and finally she edged over toward the president and said, in a clearly audible stage whisper: "Jimmy, Jimmy!"

He kept on talking.

So she tried it again, this time a little louder: "Jimmy, let's go!"

The briefing ended less than a minute later.

It was indeed fortunate the the Lord put Jimmy Carter in the governor's mansion in Atlanta for some on-the-job training before putting him in the White House, because those four years gave Rosalynn Carter on-the-job training in the duties of a first lady.

And the Carter's two campaigns to win the governorship—one lost and one successful—gave them both new expertise in politics.

As Governor Carter's reputation as an idea-man, an innovator of successful new methods in the art of government, grew and spread, state and national leaders and candidates for the presidency and other offices made a steady parade to the Atlanta Mansion. They came to learn, and they came to size him up after hearing that he was a "comer."

As official hostess at the mansion, Rosalynn met them all. She talked to them and sized *them* up, while they were sizing up her husband.

As a result of this extensive acquaintance with the political leaders of the day—an acquaintance that grew from conversations around her dinner table and in her parlor—Rosalynn was prepared with an abundance of sound advice when the idea of running for president first came to the then Governor Carter.

When I talked to her on one of the presidential campaign trips in 1976 I asked her whose idea it was that Jimmy should make a try for the White House.

She said she didn't remember who mentioned it first, or exactly when it first was mentioned. But she did recall that in their first tentative conversation about the presidency, her advice to her husband went something like this:

"Jimmy, I've talked to them all, and you are as smart as any of them, and smarter than most. I think you'd make a good president."

I reminded her that there were stories to the effect that the presidential idea was hers, and that she pushed and pushed until he finally consented to run."

Rosalynn Carter smiled and raised her eyebrows slightly.

"No, I didn't push him," she said. "Nobody pushes Jimmy."

Leaving aside the question of whose idea it was to run for the presidency, the first lady's schooling in Atlanta was important for two reasons: It taught her the art of being an extension of her husband's eyes and ears and mind, and it gave her the poise and assurance of a polished hostess.

The snobbish set in Georgetown soon learned they were not dealing with just the wife of a peanut farmer. And it wasn't long before there was a grudging admission of the elegance of her table and the tastefulness of her entertainment.

And the legion of lobbyists in the capital city was among the first to discern that, under the Carter administration, the White House was a "Mom and Pop shop."

The first lady, in fact, may have an important influence on almost anything, in any field, where the president has to make decisions.

The two of them have set up a regular, weekly "working lunch" together to discuss problems of politics and government.

She sits in on many of the foreign policy briefings, given daily to the president by his national security chief, Zbigniew Brzezinski.

When the president prepared his nationwide address on his energy policy, it was Mrs. Carter who did the final editing. She says she went over it to make sure that it would make sense to the

American people.

Mrs. Carter frequently sends sharp little notes from her office in the East Wing to her husband or his aides in the West wing. One recent note—signed simply "R"— protested against the staff piling a still heavier schedule on the president.

"Jimmy has too much to do already," she wrote. She "instructed" the aides in charge of the president's schedule to hold his commitments down.

The first lady does not always appreciate the kind of questions she gets from reporters and writers, through her East Wing office.

"It's women's page stuff," an aide snorts. "They want to know who makes her clothes, what she's going to wear for this or that affair, how Amy is holding out against the spoiling pressures of public exposure, and what she thinks about the Equal Rights Amendment. Someone who's in close touch with the president every day, is bound to resent being stuck with a lot of recipe writers."

What she seems to resent most are what she describes as "those silly questions about my clothes."

And she has told friends that she often feels like following the example of Margaret Trudeau, wife of the Canadian prime minister, who once told a reporter who was asking where she got her dresses made:

"If I were a man, would you be asking me where I got my suit made?"

Mrs. Carter also gets a bit testy when she reads in the papers that she is "the president's chief adviser."

"It makes me look cold and calculating," she complains, "and I'm not. I don't want people to think I tell him what to do. He's a very strong person and I couldn't tell him what to do even if I wanted to."

But she *does* advise the president, and she *is* the person closest to him, and reporters *will* keep on writing that way because there's a lot of truth in it. That it looks offensive to Mrs. Carter when she sees it in print isn't going to make any impression on the reporters.

The first lady also winces when the newspapers and magazines make a "big thing" out of the fact that she doesn't smoke or drink.

"They make me sound like a real prude," she says icily. "I'm not a prude!"

She adds: "Jimmy promised his father that he wouldn't smoke, and he never has. And in a strict home like mine, alcohol wasn't allowed in the house. But that doesn't make me a prude. I don't care what other people do, or say, or think, we are going to do what we feel is right. And I hope they won't call me a prude for doing it."

The Carters don't make a practice of serving whiskey to guests in the White House. They got an early start on this in Atlanta, where it was a longstanding custom that whiskey was not served in the governor's mansion.

"Besides," Mrs. Carter adds, "it saved me money."

That Mrs. Carter regards her role as first lady as an integral part of the presidency sometimes slips out accidentally in her conversation.

Talking to a friendly lady reporter on one occasion, she was asked what she was looking for, what she regarded as the most important thing in the character of the wives of the various vice-presidential candidates her husband was looking over at that time.

Her answer: "I want someone I can call on to help me with the things I'm planning to do if I get in for president." It seemed significant to the reporter that Rosalynn hadn't even noticed that she had used the word "I" in relation to the presidency.

She was asked then if she really wanted to be first lady.

"I think so," Mrs. Carter replied. "At first I was doing all this campaigning only because I thought Jimmy could be a good president. But you can't go around this country, as I have, without seeing the problems and without assuming some responsibility for solving them. I think I can make a difference."

The only first lady Mrs. Carter has ever known

was Mrs. Johnson. But, although she says she admired her and talked with her, she never asked Mrs. Johnson for any advice.

"When Jimmy was elected governor, nobody told me what to do. I picked my own jobs, with Jimmy's help," she explained. "And that's the way it is now."

At the age of fifty, Mrs. Carter has the skin and the face of a woman a decade younger. She has demonstrated, also, that she has kept most of her youthful energy.

By carefully sticking to a diet of salads and other non-fattening items during the campaign she has remained slender. Pertly pretty when young, she is still pretty, or handsome, if you prefer. She has brown hair, which she keeps short. She cuts it herself, probably one of the lingering arts she learned while she helped her widowed mother by working in a beauty parlor.

Her eyes are variously described as brown or gray-green, but leaving the color aside, they are intelligent eyes, set wide apart.

Experts in the field of feminine make-up tell me that she uses only a touch of mascara, green-beige eye-shadow, and just a little lipstick.

More important than outward appearance, those who know her best describe her as bright, honest, compassionate, spirited, well-informed, approachable, friendly and down-to-earth, with common-sense views that reflect a strong Christian upbringing.

She is, in other words, a warm, understanding human being, capable of speaking her mind when necessary, but apparently completely lacking in the guile that usually goes with being a public person.

Rosalynn Carter told me during the campaign that she prayed constantly that the Lord would reveal to her and to Jimmy his will for them.

As the campaign progressed and Jimmy Carter's chances of making it to the White House improved, month by month, they began to feel that they were moving within God's will. But still, she says, they didn't pray that the Lord would make Jimmy president, but only that his will should be done.

It was not until all the votes were in and Jimmy Carter was president-elect of the United States that the Carters were willing to concede that God must have wanted him to be president, all along.

Now their prayers are somewhat different.

The Carters—both Jimmy and Rosalynn—pray for God's guidance in every major decision. They pray together, and they pray separately several times a day.

As Christians, they are convinced that God had a particular purpose in putting them in the White House. And they have the assurance that if they remain close to God his purpose will be served.

Rosalynn

A Portrait

photo section

Rosalynn
as a young girl.

Rosalynn
in her mid-teens.

Ledger–Enquirer Newspapers

Jimmy Carter around the start of his naval career.

The newlyweds, July, 1946.

Ledger–Enquirer Newspapers

Rosalynn and Jimmy when he was a Georgia state senator.

Ledger–Enquirer Newspapers

Jeff, Jack and Rosalynn
during the gubernatorial
campaign in 1966.

Inauguration Day in Georgia, January 12, 1971.

The Carter family arrives in New York City for the Democratic Convention, July 10, 1976.

Jimmy and Rosalynn after a church service, July 25, 1976.

The Carter family, 1976.

Rosalynn Carter at home in Plains, January 15, 1977.

8

The Learner

If you get an invitation to have a meal in the family quarters of the White House, be sure to bring a book. If you don't, you may feel pretty lonely and left out of the action, because in the Carter household everybody reads at the table, even Amy. It's a family custom; always has been. And so far as their friends can figure it out, this idea of reading at the table is the net result of two strong Carter traits: a lifelong hunger for learning, which appears to be built into all of them, and an acute aversion to wasting any time. So now, with both the president and Rosalynn so intensely occupied with affairs of state, the timesaving idea of reading at the table becomes more important than ever. So don't forget that book.

"Education," says Rosalynn, "is something that comes in installments to the end of your life. When you stop learning, I think you start dying."

For Rosalynn and her husband, learning is almost an obsession. They are "suckers" for almost every mail-order course they hear about. Neighbors in Plains tell of an incident that happened shortly after they came home from the navy, when money was a very scarce item in the Jimmy Carter household.

A correspondence course in "something-or-other," they couldn't remember what, was delivered to the Carter house by the mailman, by mistake. Rosalynn opened it by mistake and showed it to Jimmy, they say, and the result was that the two of them stayed up almost all one night studying it before sending it on to the people who ordered it, the next day.

Rosalynn says even now, with her busy life in the White House, she looks back with nostalgia to their navy days, when they had time to sprawl on the floor and study things like art, music or poetry, or go out and take dancing lessons.

(Before I forget it I should give you another warning. If you get that invitation to a White House meal, and it turns out to be lunch, Mondays and Thursdays would be the best day, because Rosalynn and some friends, and some assorted members of the White House staff have Spanish lessons from nine o'clock to noon on Tuesdays,

Wednesdays and Fridays. And if it's dinner, and on Tuesday, it may end early because there's a speed-reading brush-up class Tuesday nights.)

Earlier this year the Carters set up a speed-reading class in the White House and invited all interested staffers to join. The idea was not only to make it possible for them to gulp knowledge at a faster rate, but to help Rosalynn and Jimmy save time in the process of going through the daily heap of documents, memos and letters.

The urge for learning, for self-improvement, is especially strong in Rosalynn's family, the Smiths, of Plains, Georgia.

Rosalynn herself was valedictorian of her high school class, and she joined more study clubs at school than she could readily keep up with. Her mother, Allie Smith, remembers that her elder daughter was having trouble getting her usual "A" in one course, and made her promise to wake her up every morning at five o'clock so she could study before leaving for school.

The first lady's two brothers, Murray and Jerry, each have earned two advanced degrees, and Murray, who teaches science and math in the Tri-County High School in Buena Vista, Georgia, has told a reporter that: "I'm just finished with my master's. I take a course every year. I enjoy it. I'd be a professional student if somebody would pay me for it."

Rosalynn's sister, Alethea Wall, now a housewife in Ellenwood, Georgia, says both she and Rosalynn took accounting courses early in their marriages so they could keep books for their husbands. And since then Alethea has studied and passed the examination for a state real estate license.

A friendly psychologist thinks he has it figured out. He believes it is "the Baptist brand of 'born-again' religion," which emphasizes constant study of the word of God to gain an understanding of the problems of this life and the rewards of the life after death, that first stimulated Rosalynn, and probably Jimmy, too, to a life of study.

Both of them are Bible students and Jimmy qualifies as one of the country's outstanding Bible scholars.

In a recent service at the Washington First Baptist Church, the Carters' pastor, the Rev. Charles Trentham centered his sermon on the fact that the word "disciple" means to be a "learner." Rosalynn says that her husband follows the sermons so closely that he not only follows along through the text in his open Bible, at church, but when he gets home he goes more deeply into the subject of the day's sermon by delving into Bible reference works.

The range of subjects that Rosalynn alone, and with her husband, has studied over her lifetime is almost encyclopedic. Friends say the only excuse they need to start a new course is that it covers a subject that is new to them.

Self-improvement, the acquiring of assorted kinds of knowledge, has been described as second only to their religion in importance in their lives.

With Rosalynn, it began before her marriage, and took on added interest when she found that her husband also had a hunger to learn.

There was an early course of the Great Books. Rosalynn studied during the day and coached Jimmy at night, when he returned from his navy job.

Then came a course on the Great Painters, which called for a follow-up course on art appreciation.

Jimmy had brought home from the Naval Academy a huge collection of operatic and symphonic records, so Rosalynn just about learned them by heart in the lonely days when Jimmy had sea duty.

The Spanish language has been a lifelong challenge. They started learning it in earnest, with some neighbors, when the navy sent them to San Diego. They made special trips to Tijuana to practice, and bought tapes and books to practice with. Then they took a family vacation in Mexico to make use of what they had learned.

Back in Plains from the navy, Rosalynn enrolled in a bookkeeping course, so she could manage the family business, and Jimmy took a correspondence course in farming, to brush up on the newest discoveries.

Rosalynn and Jimmy never passed up a chance to study anything, whether it was something they themselves had chosen, or something that came into their hands by accident.

Navy friends tell his story. When Carter was on active duty as an officer he was asked by a sailor under his command to order for him a correspondence course in commerical art. But by the time the course began to arrive, the sailor had been transferred. So Rosalynn, not wanting to waste this opportunity for free knowledge, launched into the lessons on charcoal drawing and painting. After practicing a week or two, she set up an easel in the backyard and managed to complete one still life—a teapot, a stick of celery and a tomato.

Then came a more intellectual exercise—a course called "The Basic Issues of Man."

Some years ago Southwestern College, in Americus, offered a course that was then called "Developmental Reading" which was the early name for what is now called "speed-reading."

The teacher, a Mrs. Leewynn Finklea, remembers that Rosalynn did well in the course, when she and Jimmy and some of their best friends in Plains came over to Americus and signed up for it. She had a meter of some kind that tested her students' progress, and she now says that if she had known that Rosalynn and Jimmy would one day be living in the White House she would have kept all their scores. She doesn't remember Rosalynn's scores, but says that Jimmy's were so sensational that she still recalls them.

When he started, she says, Carter made a score of 500 words per minute with a ninety-five per cent comprehension. Halfway through the course he had progressed so far that he was too fast for the machine to check it, and that, she says, means a speed of more than a thousand words per minute. And by the time he completed the course, she vows, the future president was reading two-thousand words per minute and still with ninety-five per cent comprehension.

The carefree days in Plains opened the door to other kinds of learning. Rosalynn and her husband were members of the Americus Country Club, and took full advantage of the club's lessons in square-dancing, ballroom dancing, jitter-bugging and the waltz.

Rosalynn, like her husband, likes classical music. But these days it's the president who has more time to listen. One of his happiest discoveries after the inauguration, he says, was to find that the executive mansion has a huge library of classical records, with a constant new supply flowing in from the record manufacturers. So now, each morning, the president selects a ten-hour classical concert—or if he is busy, his secretary does it for him—and it plays, at background music levels all day long as he works.

Rosalynn takes her husband's love of the classics so seriously that she is said to have attended a lecture on the life of Mahler, given at the Kennedy Center so they could talk about him. And their friends say she is the more serious student of music. For Carter, music is now primarily a pleasure, and not a source of learning.

At a recent formal affair at the White House, a music group from the Marine Corps was playing a selection from the classics in the White House entrance hall, as the party was breaking up. Guests were putting on their coats and the Carters were moving with them toward the front door and the stairway to the residential floors, when suddenly Carter stopped, they say, and stood as if entranced before the orchestra, his hands clasped behind him. Apparently forgetting that he was bidding farewell to his guests, the president remained motionless for almost ten minutes until the music ended, and the somewhat surprised guests, not wanting to leave without saying goodbye, took up a stand behind him. Not a soul made a move until the president came out of his reverie.

Rosalynn makes use of the White House social functions to help in her constant search for knowledge and culture.

For example, she invited to an afternoon tea Andy Warhol, Jamie Wyeth and Robert Rauschenberg. And the theatrical performances she has attended include such favorites as "Mark Twain Tonight" and "Annie."

Rosalynn is not trying to resurrect the elegance of "Camelot" days when the Kennedys ran the White House. She is not the glamour queen that Jackie Kennedy was as the White House hostess. In the white-tie-and-tails days of the Kennedys, an invitation to a White House party was almost like a summons to a royal court.

Things are more down to earth and, as a White House aide remarked, "more American and generally more relaxed and enjoyable" at the parties that Rosalynn presides over. There has even been talk that the first lady would like to put on a typical Georgia square dance in the elegant East Room, if she could find enough experienced square-dancers. If not, it would at least be a learning experience for her inexperienced guests.

Strangely for a woman in her position—a woman who seems so relaxed and at ease in the public eye, Rosalynn Carter is virtually a social loner. She's never had the time to make a lot of solid friends, she says, because she has always had to work too hard, and she was never very fond of dropping in for a cup of coffee and wasting half the day talking about unimportant things. Her husband doubles as her best friend, and she says she likes it that way.

Her only intimate women friends are still the friends of her childhood: Ruth Carter Stapleton, Jimmy's evangelist sister; Edna Langford, the mother of her daughter-in-law, Judy, and also Madeline McBean, her personal assistant.

Both Rosalynn and Jimmy Carter lean, now, toward the performing arts as their favorites. In fact, Rosalynn herself has made one successful foray into the performing field. It happened last fall, when she was asked to narrate Aaron Copland's "A Lincoln Portrait" at Constitution Hall.

Her schedule at the time didn't allow for a lot of practice. In fact, she says, she hadn't even read over the score or the text until the day of the dress rehearsal. And she claims that she was so nervous that her knees were knocking together under her long skirt, but, with Leonard Bernstein leading a full symphony orchestra behind her, she made it through the entire performance without a mistake.

Rosalynn's obsession for studying, investigating, testing, probing and learning may turn out to be one of Jimmy Carter's most valuable assets before his term as president ends. The official report she made to her husband at the end of her trip to South America as his roving ambassador has not been published, of course. But those of us in the journalistic whirl who spend a lot of time at the White House, or socializing with people who work inside the White House, are able, sometimes, to put together bits and pieces of information that reveal the shape of things happening behind the scenes. Since Rosalynn's triumphant return from the southern continent there has been a scattering of such bits and pieces. And if her findings are ever published I think I can say with some confidence that they will include these points:

1. Latin Americans' alleged admiration for Fidel Castro and for what he has done in Cuba has been exaggerated beyond all recognition in the press. Everywhere she went she found that the United States now tops the list of nations most admired by people south of the border. The "hate America" bunch shouts a lot, but is growing smaller at a rapid rate. Very few Latins believe in communism. The only thing they tend to admire about Castro is the way he stood up against the United States and got away with it, and survived and continued his development program in Cuba. The idea in the background seems to be that if he can do it, so can any other Latin country. And this could be a danger signal. It was suggested to Rosalynn that this feeling might foreshadow a wave of seizures of American investments and assets, as a way of pressuring Uncle Sam for more generous help, or better treatment in the matter of export or import quotas.

2. Some Latin American countries have high literacy rates, yet they can't seem to develop a lasting democracy. The three with the highest literacy rates, for example, are Chile, Uruguay and Argentina, and all three are now under military dictatorship. Why? Rosalynn's finding is that selfishness among the wealthy, among those who hold most of the investment capital is the basic reason for their political backwardness. Through widespread corruption, and a policy of ignoring the growing hardships of the poor, she found that these supposedly rich Latin countries had failed to build up industries of their own that were strong enough to provide even a subsistence level of living for the working class. The military became convinced that seizure of power was the only way to prevent revolution and chaos. If these military leaders can be convinced that their prosperity or rather, their country's welfare, is best served by a Bible-based policy of human rights, both economic and spiritual, there will be hope for a happier future for them. She advised her husband, therefore, that insofar as Latin America is concerned, at least, his decision to base foreign policy on human rights is on the right track.

3. Contrary to the general belief in this country, the Latin American nations do not get along well with each other and seldom, if ever, act as a bloc in world affairs on the basis of mutual good will.

They do cooperate, but only through resentment and fear of their neighbors, and usually when they discern that their economic well-being may be threatened.

4. The Latin countries do not feel any great appreciation for American grants, loans, food relief or other charity. The reason: They have a chronic unfavorable balance of trade with the United States. In 1976 the total of their collective unfavorable balances was 2.3 billion dollars, and the United States help to all of them, combined, amounted to just 300 million dollars. Thus, the Latins have good reason to believe that they are giving more economic help to the United States than this country is giving to them.

5. Rosalynn came home with a strong conviction that laziness is not a factor in the backwardness of countries to the south, in either politics or economics. The people work hard. They are poor, she is said to have reported, because they are not given a fair percentage of the wealth they produce and the answer, the only true Christian answer, is a more enlightened ruling class, willing to accept the biblical rule that "a workman is worthy of his hire."

The foregoing is in my words, but the ideas were reported to me as among those brought back by the first lady. It illustrates, I believe, why the people who know her best believe she can be of invaluable help to the president, serving as a roving extension of his own eyes, ears and mind. For what she sees and is told and what she discovers for herself on her travels is all filtered through a mind that is at once compassionate and practical, and her conclusions are drawn on the Bible-based belief that solutions for every human problem can be found in the teachings of Jesus Christ.

9

The Hostess

"Hi, everybody!" said the president of the United States, raising his right hand in a welcoming gesture. "Come on in!"

The president of Mexico and his wife, and a following of Mexican officials, bowed their thanks and shook hands with Jimmy Carter and Rosalynn as they mounted the steps under the portico at the White House entrance.

With those informal words, at the start of the Carter administration's first state dinner, on Valentine's Day, February 14, 1977, the new president set the tone for all of the state affairs that were to follow.

Under the watchful eye of the first lady and her social staff, the Carter dinners (he sometimes forgets and calls them "suppers") have been deliberately deformalized. Although the surroundings and the table settings are elegant, the social stiffness that usually goes with such a scene has been brushed aside and replaced by a relaxed, Southern-style hospitality.

And now that the initial shock has passed, the social arbiters of Georgetown have decided they like it this way, because the parties are more fun.

White House parties now start earlier (7:30 instead of 8:00 P.M.) and end earlier (11:00 P.M.) than they have under other recent presidents.

Hard liquor is not served, "because I don't want to—not because of religious reasons," says the first lady. "It's not necessary, and I'm saving the taxpayers' money," she added. State entertainment at the White House is paid for by the treasury.

After-dinner entertainment is usually by musicians or singers of world reputation. Rudolf Serkin, for example, the classical concert pianist performed at the White House recently. And sometimes, in the new spirit of informality, Rosalynn or the president will ask one of the guests to entertain, if the guest is known to be specially talented. At that very first state dinner, for example, the wife of President Jose Lopez Portillo—a former concert pianist well-known in this country and Central and South America—was asked, on the spur of the moment, by the Carters to play for the one hundred or more guests. She graciously consented—and her performance was the hit of the evening.

Rosalynn has done away with the trumpeters who used to signal the arrival of the presidential family and their guests. "Hail to the Chief" is played now, only on the arrival of the presidential family and foreign heads of state, and then only the first few bars, not the whole piece.

Rosalynn Carter insists on entertaining in a way that makes her feel comfortable. Gone are the dancing-to-the-wee-hours parties frequently given by President Ford and his wife, Betty.

White House menus are written in plain English now, not mixed French and English. A duckling when served at the White House is no longer a "canard," it's just a plain duckling.

The first lady's press secretary, Mary Finch Hoyt, says that Rosalynn and the president both put a lot of thought into their own new approach to White House ceremonial entertaining, because it not only involved protocol, but also administration policy and the image that the Carter era will be given by the historians.

She says that some of the more sophisticated guests have let it be known that they found the new style somewhat flat and even boring. But the letters the Carter family are receiving from Americans all over the country express pride in the first family's rejection of the "imperial" trappings that were building up around the presidency. The only consistent criticism, she says, was from American mothers who thought Amy should not stay up so late, just so her parents could show her off. So Amy doesn't attend so often any more, and the word has gone out that on school nights she has to go to bed by ten o'clock.

The only word for White House food—even in English—is excellent, according to dinner guests. That first state dinner consisted of shrimp gumbo, a Southern specialty, and then roast capon in grape sauce, saffron rice, asparagus tips and burnt almond ice cream. There was a choice of American wines.

Washington food service people estimate that the current White House meals would cost about $4.50 less per plate than the more exotic menus served by previous presidents' wives, so the taxpayers are getting a break, too. And the dinner-guest lists do not often rise above one hundred persons; a modest number in comparison with practices of the past; and that's another saving.

Rosalynn, daughter of a hard-working widowed mother, has never shaken the habit of being thrifty in everything—even when money might not be a prime consideration. So whenever the White House chef offers two or more suggestions for a dinner menu, Rosalynn invariably picks the one with the lowest price tag.

The guest lists made public by the White House

are a puzzle to a lot of capital old-timers. A high percentage of the names on every list are unknown, and when reporters inquire about them, it usually turns out that they are just some "folks" who put the Carters up in their homes for a night sometime in the course of the campaign, or helped other Carter relatives or campaigners. This makes it tough for the society-page writers who stand around the door trying to match faces and names.

Rosalynn has embraced the money-saving idea of inviting only half of her guests for dinner, and inviting the other half to come later for the entertainment.

The first lady seats her dinner guests at a room full of small, round tables, usually set up in the State Dining Room, with no head table—a democratic plan that appeals to the president. When the meal is over, the dinner guests move to the other end of the wide first floor hall to the East room, where they find the other half of the invited guests already seated and waiting for the entertainment to start.

President Carter is as punctual about his entertaining and his dinners as he is about his daily schedule in the Oval Office. When eleven o'clock arrives, the Carters stand up and say their farewells and go upstairs.

The president then looks over the papers on his study desk before retiring.

Only rarely do they break this routine. One such occasion came at the end of the dinner for the Canadian Prime Minister and Mrs. Pierre Trudeau. The president and his wife escorted their guests on foot down the long semicircular driveway to the Pennsylvania Avenue gate, where they said goodbye. Then they strolled slowly back up the driveway to the portico entrance, holding hands and smiling and talking together. The Trudeaus walked across the street to the Blair House.

When the British Prime Minister, James Callaghan, and his wife were their guests, Rosalynn suggested that they might like to come upstairs for awhile, after the usual eleven o'clock closing time came. So they did. And White House aides reported later that much of their twenty-minute visit was spent admiring the Carters' brand new grandchild.

Not all the White House dinners are state affairs. In fact, Rosalynn and the president find the smaller, private dinners for members of the official family more to their liking.

One of the first of these family affairs was given in early February, 1977, shortly after the inauguration, for justices of the Supreme Court and their wives.

The invitations to each individual justice said the President and Mrs. Carter would like them to drop in for dinner at 6:30 P.M.—an hour ahead of

124

the usual 7:30 beginning hour, and "casual dress" was specified.

Not until they arrived at the White House did the justices know that the full membership of the court had been invited, along with the Attorney-General, Griffin Bell, and Vice President and Mrs. Walter Mondale. The guests sat at two large round tables, the president at one of them, and the vice president at the other. Midway through the meal the president and vice president switched places, so guests at both tables would have a chance to talk to both of them.

Every administration in the past has had the Supreme Court in for a White House social get-together early in the first term, but the 1977 affair was the first one on record so completely informal. The justices and their wives had finished their meal and were on their way home by 8:30.

A meal for the administration's foreign affairs experts about a month later followed the same in-early, out-early pattern.

When foreign heads of state are entertained at the White House, diplomatic protocol demands that the guest, in return, give a dinner the next night for the president and his wife, usually at the Washington embassy of whatever nation he heads. Carter let it be known that he thinks that is just too much. And he has passed the word that he, personally, will not attend these courtesy "return" dinners. Instead, he frequently sends Rosalynn, or some other member of the Carter family (his sister, Ruth, has sat in for him, as well as his sons and daughters-in law) or Vice President and Mrs. Mondale. Carter is fanatically opposed to wasting time, and that is how he classifies this one requirement of diplomatic protocol.

Now and then, the Carters put on a real family-level dinner in their own living quarters. Guests at these more intimate affairs have included the speaker of the House, Thomas P. O'Neill, Jr. and his wife.

When Carter's Atlanta lawyer and close adviser, Charles Kirbo, was in for a meal in the family quarters, he told newsmen later that when the meal was over, the Carters excused themselves and—with Kirbo sitting in the same room watching and listening—the whole family took a speed-reading lesson before returning their attention to their guest. Later, Kirbo said, he lost a bowling match with the president in the private alley maintained for the first family's exercise.

Another favorite pastime of the first family when they have family guests in for dinner, is to top off the evening by showing a new movie in the White House projection room. The films are provided without charge by the movie industry originally at the request of the secret service, which strongly objects to presidential visits to public movie houses, because of security problems in the darkened movie auditoriums. The presidential families thus, over the years, have kept up with the latest in films without ever leaving home.

When international problems are particularly pressing, and the prime minister or chief of state of one of the nations immediately involved comes to Washington for a conference, the usual protocol is brushed aside. The president asks instead for a "working dinner," attended only by the official party of the visitor and American officials. The Japanese prime minister got the "working dinner" treatment at his own request, and so did the then Israeli Prime Minister Yitzhak Rabin.

Jimmy Carter doesn't like to "dress up." He won the argument against it at the January 20, 1977 inauguration, because it was bitterly cold and everyone (including Rosalynn) agreed that something warmer than formal attire made sense.

But the argument between Jimmy and Rosalynn goes on behind the scenes. The president detests black-tie (tuxedo) night-time parties, and the mere suggestion of white-tie-and-tails is enough to start a mini-rebellion in the White House living quarters.

Rosalynn, on the other hand, like most women, enjoys wearing pretty clothes, although she is not the fashion-model type. Rosalynn's taste leans toward the kinds of party dresses you can buy right off the rack in a good department store. It is painful for the "poor girl" of the past, who is still hidden somewhere deep down inside the first lady, to pay two hundred dollars for a party dress when a one hundred dollar dress off the rack would do just as well.

The fashion industry is worried about her attitude. A multimillion dollar business hinges on what the president's wife favors and is seen wearing. Jimmy Carter, the small businessman of Plains, knows this and sympathizes with the suffering of the fashion people when Rosalynn shows up at a dressy affair wearing a gown she has been photographed in a dozen times in the immediate past. In the days of the Kennedys, a seven hundred dollar dress was worn once, and then put away until people who notice such things had forgotten about it.

But the president has said many times his wife is doing a great job managing the family budget. Obviously, a compromise of some sort was needed to balance the anguished requests of the fashion people against the anguish of a president who admits he "he hates to spend money."

So Rosalynn set up the machinery of compromise—a sewing machine, which she used often in Plains, and even as wife of Georgia's governor. She uses it expertly, with a background of training by a mother who supported her family for years making wedding gowns and party dresses for the women of Plains, and even suits and coats for their husbands.

There were moans from the studios of dress designers when Mrs. Carter announced that, for sentimental reasons, she would wear to the inaugural balls in Washington the same blue satin gown she had worn to the inaugural celebration when her husband became the governor of Georgia, in 1970. And she did.

Rosalynn, like the majority of women, feels that what she wears is her decision. It's this bit of heresy that is causing all the fuss. Because the fashion designers point out that what the first lady wears had always been their business—and the source of a big hunk of their income.

Rosalynn is adamant of this. Her favorite styles are conservative and definitely not flamboyant. She likes covered-up designs, with raised necklines and long sleeves. Her dresses reveal her as she is. They are pretty, neat, comfortable, appropriate—and always American-made.

The first lady's clothes are watched carefully in Washington, because what she wears will influence what other women wear to the White House.

The word was passed after only two or three months of the Carter term that extravagant dresses and showy jewels were "out" for capital parties. It is to be an unadventurous era for fashions at White House functions.

Close women friends of the Carters have been putting gentle, friendly pressure on Rosalynn to do a little more in the way of "dressing up." And they have reported a little progress. Since her husband won a big boost in pay when he took over the presidency, Rosalynn has invested in several dresses designed by Dominic Rompallo and others. She does her dress shopping by secretly slipping off to New York, with one or two friends or family members and the Secret Service. She finds that she can still appear alone in public, or with a very small escort, without being recognized, in other big cities. But not in Washington.

Mrs. Carter says she has no intention of singling out any one designer as her official dressmaker, and will keep on with her "buying off the rack" except for very special occasions.

Mrs. Carter's love for doing her own sewing may irritate the fashion industry, but she gets nothing but cheers from the big pattern and fabric industries and from about 50 million other American women who share her hobby, and that includes Amy.

A photo at the top of page one of the Washington Post on Saturday, January 22, 1977, only two days after she had become the new hostess of the White House, underlined Rosalynn's relaxed informality.

There she was, in the White House foyer, dressed in a simple suit coat and skirt, greeting a long line of ladies dressed in their Sunday best. But the camera had centered on the first lady's feet, for she had kicked off her shoes, and was standing there happily wriggling her stocking-clad toes. Nobody but the photographer was taking any notice of it.

10

The Diplomat

"You know how we feel about women," said a Brazilian diplomat, with a shrug.

He had just been told that President Carter was sending his Secretary of State, Cyrus Vance, to Africa, to visit heads of state, and would send his wife, Rosalynn, to talk with Latin leaders.

"She can carry a message, I guess, as well as anybody," he said. "But if she tries to get down to serious business, she will be resented. Some may even feel insulted."

A Venezuelan who knew the Carters when Jimmy was governor of Georgia was more positive: "Sending her down here to talk about atomic bombs and human rights is the most ridiculous thing I ever heard of. She struck me as a shy, Southern lady, a housewife—nothing more."

"How can we honestly tell her how much we resent some of your policies toward us? It was her husband who set those policies! This is impossible!" said an Ecuadoran.

In Brasilia there was betting that Rosalynn would have thrown a female tantrum and flounced back home to Washington before her scheduled arrival there June 6, 1977.

It seemed, for awhile, that Rosalynn's husband also was part of a plot to make it a rough trip. On May 26, 1977, just four days before she took off on her thirteen-day, twelve thousand-mile fact-finding tour to seven countries in Latin America, President Carter signed the treaty setting aside Latin America as the world's first nuclear-weapons-free zone, an act widely resented, especially in Brazil, as an "interference" in the domestic affairs of those countries.

And on June 1, when Rosalynn was in Costa Rica on her way south, the president rubbed more salt into the wounded pride of the Brazilians by signing the American convention on human rights. This includes the proposal to create an inter-American Court of Human Rights. Brazil's government had refused to ratify the nuclear treaty or sign the human rights document.

But in the weeks before her tour started there were things going on in the White House that would change the typical Latin machismo evaluation of the lady from Plains, Georgia. For three hours every day she worked on her knowledge of Spanish, under a tutor. In between Spanish lessons she sat through more than twenty-six hours of briefings by the State Department's top Latin American experts, and by Zbigniew Brzezinski, special assistant to the president for National Security.

And just on the outside chance there was something of importance they forgot to tell her, the State Department's Latin American desk sent experts along as members of the first lady's nineteen-member entourage. They left from Brunswick, Georgia aboard an Air Force Boeing 707 dubbed the "Executive First Family," on May 30, 1977.

What had alarmed the Latins, more than anything else, was the president's announcement in his speech on May 3, that his wife was "a political partner of mine," and that she would have "substantive talks" with the leaders of Latin American countries and bring home a report on how this country can improve its relations with them. The very idea of a woman being sent on such a mission—even the wife of the president—was astounding and unsettling to the male Latin mind.

An American diplomat, just back from a long tour of duty in Brazil, explained why: "Latin women still are in the state that women were in back in the nineteenth century in Europe and the

United States. They are decorative, useful at home, but that's all. I don't think any Latin American statesman will take her seriously, even though she is the wife of the president of the United States.

"What can she discuss? Military equipment sales? Human rights? Airplane engines? She will be received with proper courtesy and the tour will be a social success, and that's all. That's my prediction."

There were some rough spots in the first few days. Rosalynn blew her cool right away when an American television reporter, with some doubtfulness in his tone, asked her why she thought she was fit to discuss serious matters with heads of state.

The first lady, her eyes flashing, and her voice trembling with suppressed indignation, said, "I think I am the person closest to the president of the United States, and if I can help him understand the countries of the world, then that's what I intend to do."

What she did not say, but what has been long apparent to newsmen in the White House, was that this trip was to be the start of the fulfillment of Carter's campaign promise that his wife was to have a "public role" as his "working partner" in government. Actually Rosalynn has been active in this role ever since the inauguration, but it was all behind the scenes; sitting in Oval Office conferences, listening to secret briefings on foreign problems, and then quietly giving the president her own opinions—which he always listens to, and sometimes accepts.

The White House made it clear just before the beginning of her trip that her role would be to ask questions and listen to the answers and bring them back to the president.

A member of the official party gave this description of her role: "The president wants to show these countries that he cares about them and is interested in their problems. He believes that the best way to do that—short of making the trip himself—is to send his wife."

And this official echoed Carter's own remark that what he was most afraid of was not that the Latin American officials would be upset that he was sending a woman, but that they would underestimate Rosalynn's capabilities.

The challenges to Diplomat Rosalynn Carter began at the very first stop, on the island of Jamaica.

Jamaica's Prime Minister, Michael Manley, a socialist of the far left, had declared publicly that he suspected capitalist Washington was plotting to overthrow him because of his friendship with Fidel Castro of Cuba. But he was cordial and more than proper when the first lady arrived, and he even told the crowd at the arrival ceremony that her husband's emphasis on human rights held forth "great encouragement."

Rosalynn later sat through seven hours of private talks with Manley. She said that she assured him United States policy toward Cuba was changing. And, as if to demonstrate that the traveling first lady knew what was in the president's mind it was announced in Washington only four days later that there would be an exchange of diplomats with Cuba, as the first step toward resuming full relations.

She also told Manley her country was concerned over the island's social problems. To underline her concern, she visited the Kingston slums and inspected two social service centers. And she made a hit with the crowds along the way by embracing a small girl who broke through the police lines and hugged her legs, and then took Rosalynn's hand and walked with her and chatted for several blocks.

In Costa Rica, the second stop, the first lady demonstrated she had learned the art of avoiding direct answers and flat promises. President Daniel Oduber Quiros asked her to intercede to have the United States quota on Costa Rican beef increased.

"I couldn't promise you anything that we could not deliver," she said.

And at the next stop, in Quito, Ecuador, Rosalynn calmly informed the military government that her country was most unlikely to lift the trade restrictions that were imposed after Ecuador raised its oil prices, in step with other OPEC countries.

When the Ecuadorans pressed another of their complaints, protesting the United States ban on the sale by Israel to Ecuador of Israeli-made Kfir jets with American-made engines, Rosalynn was ready for it.

Her husband, she said, stopped the sales because he did not want to see such sophisticated weapons introduced into the area.

When the Ecuadorans argued that they needed the planes because Peru, their enemy of longstanding, already had sophisticated weaponry, Rosalynn promised to do what she could to influence the Peruvians to slow down the pace of their military buildup.

And on arrival in Lima on June 3 she spent nearly three hours closeted with President Francisco Morales Bermudez. Her staff said they talked mainly about the alarm their arms build-up was causing in Ecuador, and ways that the tension might be alleviated.

Meanwhile, the tour was getting a little rough. In Quito, Ecuador—elevation nearly ninety-five hundred feet—Rosalynn was given oxygen twice to relieve her of the effects of the altitude.

And as the first lady was winding up her talks in Quito about 150 students put on a noisy demonstration against Yankee imperialism. A couple of Molotov cocktails were thrown, and the police answered with tear gas, but there was never any personal danger to the visitor. The demonstrators were kept about a hundred yards away from her motorcade.

At every stop—especially those where officials were known to be hostile to any American policies—Rosalynn urged them to talk freely to her, and assured them she could take anything they had to dish out.

"You can be blunt," she would say. "Go ahead and tell me what's on your mind. That's what I'm here for."

Later, at her last stop, in Venezuela, President Carlos Andres Perez, told the press that he had been "pleasantly surprised" by this "extraordinary woman," and that other governments along the line said the same in messages to him.

Even in Brazil, where Rosalynn Carter's party nervously predicted trouble, and where the government was strongly hostile to the United States' nuclear and human rights stands, Brazilian officials, at the wind-up of her visit, described their official American visitor as "poised and well-briefed" for her meetings with Brazilian President Ernesto Geisel. A diplomat in the Brazilian capital of Brasilia, summed up the general opinion of Rosalynn this way: "This lady knows what she's talking about. She asks the right questions and she knows the right answers.

There's no fooling around."

The Brazilians resented Carter's opposition to their plans to buy extensive nuclear fuel facilities abroad. And the first lady explained in detail to the Brazilian president why her husband is concerned about the proliferation of nuclear capability on the South American continent.

A part of her assignment in Brazil was to make it unmistakably clear that President Carter had no intention of altering or compromising on his decision to base his foreign policy on human rights, despite the danger this policy might disrupt relations with some countries other than Brazil, whose relations with the United States already had plummeted to the lowest point of the thirteen years of military rule in Brasilia.

The negative turn of relations with Brazil was worrisome both to the United States government (especially the military) and to American business because Brazil always before has been our strongest political and economic ally in Latin America. In return, Brazil had enjoyed a growing inflow of American capital, and a prosperous exchange of goods—especially coffee—with the United States.

There were charges of bad faith on both sides. Some American politicians were making hay with their coffee-drinking constituents by blaming the Brazilian government for "rigging" the high prices of coffee.

On the Brazilian side, in addition to resentments over the human rights policy and U.S. moves against Brazil's plans to build a chain of nuclear power plants, there was worry over American labor unions' demands for cuts in the imports of Brazilian shoes and textiles.

And Washington deplored President Geisel's apparent move away from his former policy of moderate political liberalism, when he announced that foreign books and magazines arriving in Brazil's post offices would be censored.

Still another blow to relations was the announcement that the U.S. Steel Corporation, which had discovered one of the world's largest iron ore deposits in northeastern Brazil, had announced it would not take part in developing the discovery. It did not announce its reasons.

Ambassador Rosalynn stayed three days in Brazil. It was her longest stopover of the tour. And she went out of her way one day to speak up for human rights and to demonstrate her own personal political courage.

She told her Brazilian hosts that she wanted to meet personally with two American missionaries who had been held in jail by the Brazilians on what were described as trumped-up charges, and treated cruelly.

The missionaries—the Rev. Lawrence Rosebaugh, 42, a Catholic priest, and Thomas Capuano, 24, a Mennonite—told her they had been treated "like animals." They were held in a filthy cell, they said, and were mistreated physically.

They had been working among the poor of Brazil.

"I have listened to their experiences, and I sympathize with them," Mrs. Carter told reporters after talking with the missionaries for about fifteen minutes. "I have a personal message to take back to Jimmy."

Brazilian officials maintained a discreet silence. Her visit to the missionaries seemed calculated to underline her husband's determination to let the Brazilians know that they had the power to improve or to worsen their relations with America by their handling of human rights from that point on.

One of the first lady's prime assignments was to find out, it she could, in her series of Latin "mini-summits," what the Carter administration is doing right, and what it is doing wrong in the Latin countries.

Whether or not she achieved this goal was known only by President Carter, who got reports from her daily by phone and personally when the trip ended.

Eight days after she returned from her tour of South America, Rosalynn was in San Jose, California, and she used that occasion to make her first, and only, public report on what she had learned and what she said and did. It was a speech that covered probably all that the public would be told of the venture, but—more important—it gave a rare insight into the first lady's character, her thinking and the extent of her partnership with her husband, the president. Here are the highlights of what she said:

"Jimmy and I have long had an interest in Latin America. We have traveled in Central and South America, have many friends there, and we've studied Spanish for as long as I can remember. Jimmy is fluent—I am not, but I try—and Jimmy thought a trip to Latin America at this time was important for several reasons.

"First, at the beginning of every new administration, foreign governments want and need to understand the new president, who he is and what he cares about. And we want to know the same about other leaders. Jimmy thought it was important for a personal representative to convey to the leaders of these countries a sense of the goals and priorities of the Carter administration.

"Second, he had made three major speeches on foreign affairs: one to the United Nations, one to the Organization of American States, and one at Notre Dame. These needed to be explained, firsthand, to the heads of state, particularly our approach to Latin America and the Caribbean, and our position on major issues, such as human rights and nuclear proliferation, and he wanted their frank views and their comments about these speeches and the direction of his policies.

"Third, as I felt I could establish a personal relationship between these leaders and my family, which is very important, he asked me to go. . . .

"I had hours of briefings. I learned the history of the United States' relations with each country I was to visit. I learned current issues. I studied the OAS speech and the Notre Dame speech. I really had a lot to learn.

"The diplomatic language, for example, is a whole new vocabulary. For instance, I was in Venezuela, the last country, and in my arrival statement I said that we valued our 'special relationship' with that country. Do you know, 'special relationship' is the worst thing I could have said. [To them] it denotes 'paternalism,' which is exactly the opposite of the relationship we want with the Caribbean and Latin American countries. "The main theme of our foreign policy as applied to Latin America and the Caribbean is: a respect for the sovereignty and recognition of the individuality of all governments. All of the countries are different. We recognize it. For too long we have lumped them all together and had one Latin American policy. That's like having one policy for everyone in this room. Every leader I spoke with was very pleased that we are recognizing their uniqueness. . . ."

Human Rights

"We are committed to the advancement of human rights throughout the world, and Jimmy's definition of human rights is a broad one. It doesn't mean freedom from political oppression only, but freedom from hunger and a right to the basic needs of life—political, social and economic rights.

"And, also, he doesn't believe this is only our concern, but a global concern. We must join with every nation of the world and work together toward the goal of assuring the basic human rights of all people, everywhere.

"We must end the spectre of war and waste of armaments, nuclear and conventional. We have a commitment to work with developing countries in searching for ways to narrow the gap between the developed and the developing countries.

"With these things in mind, I'd like to give you some impressions of the countries I visited."

Jamaica

"This is a beautiful country. . . [but its] problems are typical of those of the new and developing countries of the Caribbean. They need help, but they feel they have been ignored.

"Prime Minister Manley explained to me his belief in democratic socialism—that all Jamaicans should share in the benefits of the country's economic development and that political freedom must be preserved.

146

"We need to search for ways to cooperate with them on trade issues, for instance, and we must express in international meetings our genuine concern for their problems."

Costa Rica

"Costa Rica is a democracy. They have no army. They have been able to spend their money on the development of their country. Their educational system is excellent. Ninety-six percent of their citizens are literate. I visited a school and watched mentally retarded and deaf children perform in a wonderful physical education program.

"I asked about services for the mentally afflicted, and the teacher told me that there is a place in a school for every single child. Costa Rica has been an important leader in human rights. The American Convention on Human Rights was negotiated in San Jose [Costa Rica] in 1969. [It] is an agreement among the members of the OAS that human rights will be respected and guaranteed in their countries. Costa Rica and Colombia were the two countries of those I visited who had already signed and ratified this agreement. I spoke to all the other leaders about it. Venezuela announced that they had ratified it the day after I left."

Ecuador and Peru

"[These] ... are two countries which have military governments now, but which are committed to reestablishing democratic and civilian governments. Both countries are working on plans.

"In Ecuador, very soon, the people will be voting on a constitution. They are already registering their people to vote, alphabetically, and they told me they were in the 'S's.

"This is a troubled area, and we are concerned about the arms build-up. Peru, for instance, is bordered by five different countries. Ecuador is one of them. Chile, Bolivia, some of these countries historically have been adversaries, and so they feel a need for defense.

"When one arms, the others have to arm. . . . The leaders of these countries are struggling with the problem. They are sincere and very concerned. They would much prefer to spend their own limited financial resources on developing their countries. In fact, one official said to me: 'If we didn't have to buy armaments and could spend our money on education of our people, it would be the best possible thing that could happen to our country.'

"But they have to feel secure. How can a way be worked out so that they can feel secure without arming? Through a strengthened OAS? Through the United Nations? I don't know. But we explored several alternatives. It is very important to pursue. It could avoid the arms build-up and war.

"In Peru, I visited some experimental

situations—potatoes and guinea pigs. . . ." [The first lady told her small audience, mainly women, that Latin America, with the proper equipment, could do a lot toward feeding the hungry of the world. And then she continued the story of her trip:]

"Under our Trade Act of 1974 we gave tariff preferences to the developing countries for many of their exports. We excluded the OPEC countries. Ecuador and Venezuela have oil and are members of OPEC. Therefore, they are excluded from these trade preferences—even though they did not participate in the oil embargo and have always been reliable sources of petroleum for us.

"In fact," she went on, "they kept us supplied with petroleum during the oil embargo of 1973, and they resent very much that this exclusion applies to them. . . .

"My own personal opinion (and I'm not speaking for Jimmy or the administration) is that this amendment should be changed. . . ."

Brazil

"Brazil is the largest country I visited, both in land and population. There is always a very large reserve of good will in Brazil for the United States. They fought with us [beside us] in World War II and have historically been our friends.

"An important issue which Brazil confronts, and which confronts the whole world, is how to have nuclear energy without risking the spread of nuclear explosive capability. Brazil must have nuclear energy—they import more than eighty percent of their oil. We want them to have this energy. But we would hope that they could have it without a reprocessing facility which would give them nuclear explosive capability. . . .

"Latin America has the opportunity to be a model for the whole world—a nuclear-free zone. There is an agreement called the Tlatelolco Treaty which, if put into effect would do just that, make Latin America and the Caribbean a nuclear-weapons-free zone. Most of the countries have signed. Brazil has signed with certain conditions. We hope they will waive these conditions."

Colombia

"Colombia is a democracy. We have much in common and feel very close to the Colombians. But right now, we and Colombia have a problem with drug-trafficking. The drug situation in Mexico is greatly improved. Our governments have collaborated, and the work we have done together is paying off.

"We need to work together, now, with the government of Colombia in the same spirit of cooperation. I spoke to the president very frankly about it, and he agreed with me that it is a mutual concern."

Venezuela

"[This was] the last country I visited, [and] it is a great friend and ally. They're working together with us to promote human rights, to halt nuclear proliferation, and in many other areas, and President Perez has taken a leadership position on these and other important issues.

"I left Latin America with an overwhelming sense of kinship with the persons I had met and with friendships that will be lasting, and with a feeling of great willingness, yes, eagerness to cooperate [in an unrestrained way] to solve the problems that confront us.

"The Caribbean and Latin countries have traditionally been our friends and allies. We need and want their counsel and support in problems that face not only their countries—but [also] this nation and the world.

"We need to consult closely with them on matters such as trade, finance, technology, investment and development assistance. And we need to work closely with them on our common purposes of human rights and the maintenance of peace.

"We need to strengthen our cultural relations. They have contributed so much to our music, drama and art. After all, the first settlers of Georgia and California were Spanish-speaking!

"As we examine the world and its problems," she said in closing the review of her first substantive diplomatic assignment, "it is very important to hear the wisdom of our neighbors to the south. It is not so far from San Jose, Costa Rica, to San Jose, California."

The professionals of the State Department were impressed by the first lady's approach to problems on her Latin tour, and especially by the uncomplicated, direct language she used in getting her ideas across to those she talked with.

Having struggled, herself, through years of trying to become fluent in Spanish, she had a feeling for the need to use simple English words and speak slowly to these Spanish-speaking leaders who must have found the English language more confusing and difficult than she found Spanish.

In any case, the diplomatic "pros" in Washington pronounced the first lady's "trial by diplomacy" a complete vindication of her husband's judgment in sending his wife as his representative.

And there is a general feeling that her performance may have changed a lot of *macho* Latin minds about what a woman can do, if given the opportunity. The president's wife came home hoping that her diplomatic venture, and the complete success that it scored, will also open the door to more women diplomats in this country's diplomatic corps.

One "old pro" among the American diplomats

may have hit the core of the whole matter when he commented: "It's obvious, now, that the secret of success in diplomatic confrontations is to send a pretty woman with brains. They're bound to be courteous to her, and that will minimize and cool the debate. And they are bound to accept her statements of the real American policy—especially if she happens to be the wife of the president."

11

The Work

It may be a source of comfort to Mr. Average American to know that even the president of the United States gets tangled up in red tape, and, now and then, is completely frustrated by it. President Carter lost his first encounter with it on February 17, 1977. It was on that date that he had proposed to appoint his wife, Rosalynn, as "chairperson" of the President's Commission on Mental Health. Everyone concerned agreed that it was a logical, appropriate and proper appointment, because of the first lady's four years of experience in mental health work while her husband was governor of Georgia. Everyone agreed, that is, except the Office of Legal Counsel of the Department of Justice. On the very day that she had hoped to be appointed and start to work at the job she had looked forward to, Mrs. Carter received a little note from the Legal Counsel's office. It read:

"The law prohibits the president from appointing a close relative, such as a wife, to a civilian position."

President Carter got on the phone to the lawyers and to Justice, insisting there must be a loophole. "There always is," he said. But there wasn't.

"A civilian position," said the legal voice on the phone, "may be unpaid as well as paid. So the fact that Mrs. Carter is not going to be paid for her work does not alter the situation. Justice has determined that all of the twenty members of the commission, including the chairperson, will in fact be serving in civilian positions. Therefore, the prohibition against the appointment of the president's wife still holds."

In the end, a grumbling chief executive had to bow and compromise. Rosalynn was given the privilege of doing the work, without the title. The Justice Department has finally acknowledged that "there is no problem with your designation of Mrs. Carter as honorary chairperson."

"So I am going to be a very active honorary chairperson," she told questioners later. "We already have office space in the Executive Office Building, which is very close. I will be spending many hours a week there. I will be traveling. I will be involved in the fact-finding process, going around the country for hearings in the next six months. I intend to be active."

"Why," she was asked, "were you never asked to head the mental health program in Georgia? You say you worked in mental health there, but there's no record that you were ever the head of the state program."

"Don't get the wrong impression," Mrs. Carter replied quickly. "I didn't know anything about mental health programs or problems at all, when Jimmy was elected governor, so I didn't want to be in charge of the program in Georgia. I had never worked in the field. But during our first year in the governor's mansion I worked as a volunteer in a number of regional mental hospitals. And I learned about mental sickness by working firsthand with those who were sick. I think that I now have the knowledge and experience to do the job."

"Honorary chairperson" in the planning of nationwide mental health programs is the only formal title Rosalynn had acquired in her first year, but it doesn't even hint at the range of her active interests.

She is actively lobbying for better treatment of the elderly in America.

She is pressing Congress at every chance she gets to set up a system of day-care centers for the children of working mothers.

She is spearheading the way through red tape for a brand new program—which was not yet officially in existence in the early fall of 1977—a program to rescue the frustrated young people of the big city ghettos and give them an education so their lives will not be wasted.

She is using her influence to get the Equal Rights Amendment moving forward again, through the state legislatures. It was stalled for months, tantalizingly close to enactment.

She is trying to whip up enthusiasm for a national "friendship force," an idea that was born in Georgia while Carter was governor, and is still alive and active. The idea is to have each state in this country choose a foreign country and arrange to exchange "friendship" visits by planeloads of visitors with its chosen country, on a regular schedule. Georgia chose Brazil.

She has lent her support to charitable projects of the First Baptist Church in Washington, D.C., one aimed at helping outpatients of local mental hospitals, and another which supplements the income of the aged who live in poverty, and helps get medical attention for them.

Besides all this, of course, there is the job of supervising everything that takes place in the White House—a job that falls to every president's wife. She plans state dinners and receptions, entertains visiting notables, helps the president make social contacts with members of Congress.

And there is the never-ending flow of thousands of letters, including forty to fifty invitations every day. They all have to be considered, and answered.

Mrs. Carter had a paid staff of eighteen in her offices in the White House East Wing. But they were soon swamped, and the call went out for volunteers to answer phone calls, type letters, read mail, keep track of invitations and answer inquiries from reporters.

Then there are those one-shot affairs that take a lot of planning before they happen, and follow-up work afterward. An example: The White House Conference on Ageing, held in May, 1977. It was "Rosalynn's baby," said an aid.

The first lady was the featured speaker at an early summer plenary session of the National Council of Ageing at the Capital Hilton Hotel in Washington. Mother Bernadette de Lourdes, the Carmelite nun who introduced her told the audience that "she could turn out to be the most socially active first lady since Eleanor Roosevelt."

As if to demonstrate the truth of Mother Bernadette's words, Rosalynn flew off to Chicago the next day to preside at the first meeting of the President's Commission on Mental Health, and to inspect a model community health clinic operating there.

Bouncing back to Washington she went into conference with the President's Committee on

Mental Retardation, where she asked for specific suggestions that could be worked into legislation to give the families of the mentally retarded the kind of help already being given to families of alcoholics.

She proposed the training of professionals to work with both the retarded and their families, and to educate the public so as to dispel the stigma that surrounds retardation because of ignorance.

She warned committee members that the best way to get action out of Jimmy Carter was to "be brief."

"If you give Jimmy specific, brief, understandable recommendations," she said, "you increase your chances of getting action. He hates the sight of huge reams of text."

When you read of new ideas announced by the president in the field of physical or mental health, the odds are about ten to one the idea was Rosalynn's.

Maybe it's supposed to be a secret, but he first "cleared with Rosalynn" the proposal he sent to Congress on April 25, 1977, to slow the spiraling of health costs by putting a lid on hospital spending.

The bill would fix a tight limit of nine percent on the yearly increases of charges by individual hospitals.

For future study, the first lady and the president have proposed that there be established a fixed fee schedule for doctors, that tighter controls be clamped on nursing homes and chronic disease hospitals, including mental hospital, and that general hospitals give more attention to expanding their out-patient services, and thus reduce the number of costly hospitalizatons.

On top of all these wide-ranging national interests, Rosalynn expects to get more assignments as roving personal representative and ambassador for the president.

Carter made no secret of his delight at the success of his wife's first attempt at diplomacy in Latin America. He didn't say what the next foreign assignment would be, but he assured newsmen that "we'll be doing this some more."

It's the kind of an outlook that should delight the heart of a first lady who told one interviewer that she "can't sit still without having something in my hands to do."

There'll be a lot of domestic travel for her, on the president's behalf, too.

"It's going to be very hard for Jimmy to travel in our country and talk to people and find out how they feel about the way things are going," she said.

"But I can travel and bring back to him my impressions of what's happening." What she didn't add was that Jimmy has great respect for his wife's impressions, thinks she has a "great mind" and probably a better political feel for things than he has.

Rosalynn has told friends that an important part of her job is to keep track of the promises Jimmy made during the campaign. And, with her husband involved deeply in foreign affairs most of the time, she sees it as her duty to remind him now and then when the proper moment comes to fulfill some particular promise.

One hard and fast determination in the first lady's mind is that in the mental health field, and in the search for new ways to help the elderly, there will be no wasted effort through duplication of studies already made by past administrations.

"I know," she said in a speech to the National Conference on the Ageing on April 18, 1977, "that there are many programs already for the elderly. The concern I have is that these programs do not reach the people they are supposed to reach. There is no coordination between programs.

"Millions of our old people don't even know these programs are available to them," she said, and indicated that her first priority would be to find ways to see that the elderly find out that no more waiting for help is necessary, that all they need to do is ask for it in many cases.

The final link between the elderly and the programs set up for them, she added, is to make it easy for them to find out "where to go when they need help."

"I am determined that the White House will be open and available for help to the aged."

Mrs. Carter, at one point during the presidential campaign, was guest speaker at a meeting of the National Conference on the Ageing. In the spring of 1977, as the first lady, she accepted a return engagement.

She told them she became aware of the tragedy of idleness and loneliness among the elderly by firsthand experiences with her own mother, Allie Smith, and the president's mother Lillian Carter.

It is a real tragedy, she said, when an elderly person is able to go on working and wants to work, but cannot find employment, and just sits, with nothing to do.

"My mother was retired from the post office at the age of seventy, and it was a traumatic experience for her.

"Jimmy's mother rather than remain idle, joined the Peace Corps at sixty-eight and went to India to make use of her talents as a nurse—you are familiar with that—she was miserable at home doing nothing.

"Besides this experience, firsthand, I traveled for a year and a half campaigning, asking people to vote for my husband. I was in convalescent homes, nursing homes, golden age clubs. . . . There is no way you can do that, like I did, talk with people, see their needs and their problems, without becoming involved with them and without developing a responsibility for them.

"I told them then that if Jimmy was elected president, that I would work to help solve the problems of the elderly, and I intend to do that.

"Now because of all these visits to the elderly, I have people that are just reaching out to me for help. I get about three thousand letters a week, many of them from elderly citizens; many from children who are concerned about the high cost of hospital care, the cost and poor quality of nursing homes for their parents; many from neighbors and friends of older persons who watched this past year as old people struggled to stay warm, to have decent clothes, decent food to eat, to try to pay their bills and not to be a burden to anybody."

She read to the huge gathering some sample paragraphs from typical letters that come from the ageing.

The first, she said, was from a man in Roswell, New Mexico, who wrote:

"I am seventy years old, and have been retired since age sixty-five, which was according to company policy. I didn't want to retire because I was in good health, and I wanted to go on working. I have education, experience, know-how and am still in good health, but no one will give me an opportunity to work. I have never applied for, or accepted, any welfare aid. All I want is responsible work."

Another, she said, came from a man in Henford, California, and pointed up another kind of problem for the older citizens:

"I am seventy-six years of age, and my property taxes were increased one-third over last year. I get a $220 Social Security pension check each month, and it would take five months of these checks just to pay my property taxes."

A woman in Cincinnati, Ohio, wrote Mrs. Carter:

"I am a widow, seventy-six years old. I have had open heart surgery and a stroke. My husband's pension did not provide for me. My prescription drug medicine is terribly expensive, and I have to do without many necessities to pay for it."

"Then listen to this one," the first lady said. "This one really touched me." It was from a woman in New Hampshire. She wrote:

"I am elderly, live on an income of $184 a month, try to maintain my home and be active in helping others in the same situation. I see so many in want, living in small apartments, shut off from life, with no activity to help them prolong their lives.

"If I had the means I would buy abandoned farms here in New Hampshire and let the active elderly, such as myself, maintain them. I would give them an incentive to live, and would be useful to the state of New Hampshire. Several elderly people could live together on one of these farms.

How much happier they would be to be needed and be busy, than to be left alone in a dreary apartment."

Mrs. Carter added that the letter ended with these words: "Thank you for reading my dream."

The first lady paused a moment, and then declared: "I believe that I can spotlight these needs, draw attention to them, focus the eyes of the country on the needs of the elderly."

Rosalynn's "secret project"— which seemed at the time to be a open secret around the White House—began to leak out to the public in July, 1977.

The leakage began when people started asking about a new face that had shown up in the Executive Office Building , a man who was given an office there by the White House, with no announcement of what he was to handle.

His name, it was discovered, was Bill Milliken, a Christian youth worker who had run a highly successful program to combat drug abuse when Carter was governor of Georgia.

It was learned, moreover, that Milliken was one who had shared an intimate "life in Christ" with Governor Carter. He was one of a small group of Georgians the governor called upon frequently to share his spiritual burdens. Another in the group was the lawyer who is now counsel to the president, Robert Lipshutz, member of the Jewish faith who, in spite of religious differences, maintained a deep spiritual affinity with Carter and his Christian friends.

The word finally leaked out that Milliken had come to the White House with a new plan for rescuing troubled youth. And through the influence of Mrs. Carter the president had decided to give him an opportunity to work out the details in the Executive Office Building, and give it at least a trial run.

What Milliken was drafting was a prototype national program which he calls "Project Propinquity," which sounds more like a "cover" than a description of what is in the wind. From scattered sources it became fairly clear that the aim of the program was to rescue youth from the ghetto environment and see that they get the training that will motivate them to go straight and do well in society.

Already under way in the Bronx, in Atlanta and other scattered cities, under a program financed by Christian businessmen and other private sources including the Lilly Foundation, and directed by a Christian group called "Young Life," Milliken's program now is to have the joint sponsorship of the federal government also.

Through the patronage of the first lady, Milliken was invited to private sessions at the White House the president was favorably

impressed with his ideas, and an interdepart-
mental committee was set up with 2.7 million
dollars of federal money to spend.

"I have asked the department heads to see him
[Milliken]," Mrs. Carter said, because I think what
he's doing is so important. We spend money,
money, money on these problems, and so many of
the services don't even reach the people who need
them. I also think it's important to get the private
sector involved, and Bill does, too. I think what he
does is just great, and he's so unselfish."

By mid-July, 1977, it was said, the the prospects
were that the federal government's 2.7 million
dollars would be matched by state, local and
private sources, and that the funds would be
poured into the expansion of pilot "Propinquity"
programs already under way in New York,
Atlanta and Indianapolis.

Mrs. Carter gave a giant-size push for private
financing in May, 1977 it is learned, by sponsoring
a breakfast for the thirty-five-year-old Milliken,
attended by 230 businessmen. It gave him a
chance to outline his program to them and solicit
their support.

Whispers were that with Mrs. Carter clearing
away obstacles, Milliken hoped to get his
youth-rescue projects under way in seven more
cities within a year. The likely cities: Hartford,
Minneapolis-St. Paul, Pittsburgh, Los Angles,
Houston, Fayetteville, N.C., and Washington,
D.C.

The secret of Milliken's success, one reporter quipped, is the "three F's"—Faith, Fund-raising and First Lady.

Mrs. Carter tells this story about how she first became interested in the problems of mental health. Campaigning with her husband who was running for governor of Georgia in 1970, "I had so many people ask me what will you do for my retarded child, or I have a son in the seventh grade who is emotionally disturbed and I don't know where to go to get help for him. What will your husband do if he is elected governor?' "

She found that mental health problems touched the lives of many more people than she had realized, and then, after hearing of so many of these problems "one day I decided that I wanted to work with the mental health program when Jimmy was governor.

"I was campaigning in a little community in Georgia. I had a reception at six o'clock in the afternoon. When I got through with the reception I was through for the day, and I found out that Jimmy was going to be in that same town that night—which was great. I never saw him in the campaign.

"So I stayed, and got in the back of the auditorium while he spoke. After the speech was over, I got in line, went down with everybody else, and shook hands with him. He shook my hand before he saw who I was, and then he said: 'What are you doing here?' And I said I came to see what you are going to do about the mental health program in Georgia.

"He said: 'We are going to have the best one in the United States, and I am going to put you in charge of it.'

"Well, he didn't put me in charge of it, of course. But he did appoint me to the governor's commission to improve services to the mentally and emotionally handicapped.

"So, in my campaign biography (when Carter ran for president) I had a little paragraph that said I was interested in mental health. So, everywhere I went, if the people there had a good program, they wanted me to see it. I had a good chance to see things happening all over the country that are good. I also saw things happening that I thought needed help."

The first lady says that only forty percent of the population is being reached now by the federally aided community centers for mental health.

Her Commission on Mental Health had only $100,000 of federal money to start its work. It is soliciting private help, and the executive order that established it called for the "cooperation of other federal agencies."

"I have learned, working with the programs in Georgia," Mrs. Carter said, "that it doesn't take extra-large sums of money, sometimes it just takes a redistributing of the funds that are already available."

With the help of "great volunteers, who give us their services day after day after day, and the professional people who want to see things done," she added "if we can all meet together, and pull together all these plans that are moving in different directions . . . we have a chance to do great things!"

12

The Moralist

Teddy Roosevelt was right! The exuberant Rough Rider of the early 1900s was the first president to perceive fully the potential moral influence of the White House, and he proclaimed it "a bully pulpit!" And in the decades since he rode off into history, it has become more and more clear that what the president and his family say—and, even more important, what they do—has a significant influence on the life-style and the thinking of millions of Americans. That influence has been strongest in the area of morality.

When Jimmy Carter was asked during the campaign why he, a devoutly religious man, did not choose the ministry instead of politics, as a career, he replied, "The presidency gives me a

173

chance to magnify whatever influence I have, for either good or bad, and I hope it will be for good. I don't look on it with religious connotations, but it gives me a chance to serve."

The first lady, in different words, said the same things. Asked by a reporter if she was concerned by the public criticism she was getting because two of her married sons and their wives had come to live in the White House, she answered, "Oh, no! Not at all. It doesn't cost the public anything to have them here, and I think the unity of our family will be good for the country to see."

She added that her sons do worry a little about the criticism, because they don't want people to think they are living off the government—which they are not—but she sees one overriding advantage in the arrangement.

"Jimmy is at home more here in the White House, than he ever has been before, and I think it is good for the family to be together, so they can give each other more love and comfort and moral support. This kind of unity in the family that lives in the White House," she emphasized, again, "is good for the country."

It was in the early weeks in office that the president demonstrated the Carters' concern for family unity and stability, especially in the families of his top executives in government. In February, 1977, the following memo, written on presidential stationery and signed, "J. Carter," was circulated among the staff and Cabinet members:

"I am concerned about the family lives of all of you. I want you to spend an adequate amount of time with your husbands, wives and children, and also to involve them, as much as possible, in our White House life. We are going to be here a long time, and all of you will be more valuable to me and the country with rest and a stable home life. In emergencies we'll all work full time. Let me have your comments."

It was on February 10, in a talk before workers at the Department of Housing and Urban Development, that the president made his now most famous remark on the family and marriage.

"It is becoming more and more of a problem in holding families together, to have some flexibility in the times that people work," he said. "I have asked my own White House staff, and I've also asked Pat Harris and other Cabinet members to protect the integrity of their own families.

"I think it is very important that all of us in government not forget that no matter how dedicated we might be, and how eager to perform well, that we need a stable family life to make us better servants of the people." And then he made his most widely quoted ad lib:

"So those of you who are living in sin, I hope you'll get married. Those of you who have left your spouses, go back home. And those of you who don't remember your children's names, get reacquainted.

"I think it's very important that we have stable family lives. And I am serious about that."

There was scattered, nervous laughter, at first, and then a burst of enthusiastic applause when the full weight of what the president had said sunk in.

In the White House pressroom there was joking about the use of the biblical term "living in sin," but no amount of research could turn up any parallel occasion when a president had spoken so frankly on a subject that "nobody talks about," and that needed an airing so much.

Reaction was not long coming.

The very next day there were editorials all over the country, almost all of them praising the president for lifting the veil from a subject that was causing so much worry, moral decay and eventual misery.

And in the White House, a presidential aide who was known to have been "living in sin" for nearly five years, promptly and publicly married the lady.

In a news conference on June 30, 1977, the president again faced a pointed question on sexual morality. Again, his answer came straight from the Bible. "Mr. President," the questioner began, "do you ever hold it against people in your organization who are involved promiscuously with other women?"

The president: "I've done everything I could

properly and legitimately do to encourage my staff members' families to be stable, and I have also encouraged the same sort of thing in my Cabinet. If there are some who have slipped from grace, then I can only say that I'll do the best I can to forgive them and pray for them."

It used to be common knowledge in this country that when a politician got a divorce he was committing political suicide. This was especially true in presidential politics. Nelson Rockefeller's divorce was a factor in his failure to win the nomination in 1968. Adlai Stevenson, divorced, lost miserably in 1952, and again in 1956.

But somewhere along the line the public's attitude changed. Though the undivorced and closely affectionate Carters won in 1977, the ballot at the national level was heavy with divorced people: Betty Ford, Ronald Reagan, Robert Dole, Eugene McCarthy. And there was Vice President Rockefeller in the outgoing administration.

As the nation's divorce rate soared, political figures seemed to be leading the rush to the courts. At least, their domestic failures drew the publicity. Cabinet members, congressmen, ambassadors and White House staff people severed their marriage ties as freely as the rest of the population: Senators Herman Talmadge of Georgia, John Tower of Texas, Lowell Weicker of Connecticut, and Don Riegle of Michigan. And the Congressional sex scandals underlined the moral decline, with disgrace coming to such highly honored figures as Congressman Wayne Hays of Ohio and Wilbur Mills of Arkansas. Watergate was the symptom of a disease already far advanced.

The nation's divorce rate had risen from three divorces for every ten marriages in 1966 to one divorce for every two marriages in 1976.

Between 1970 and 1976, according to Commerce Department statistics, the number of unmarried couples living together rose from 327,000 to 660,000, and in 1975, 14.3 percent of the country's births were illegitimate, whereas in 1960 only 5.3 of the new babies were produced by unmarried mothers.

What happened to bring on this explosion of immorality?

For fifteen years, from 1945 to 1960, the families living in the White House were examples of domestic tranquility and stability. There was never a breath of scandal in the lives of Harry and Bess Truman. The worst that was said was that Harry failed in the haberdashery business. And in the Eisenhower years, the one whispered rumor of infidelity was unconfirmed, and the public display of affection by Ike and Mamie during their eight years in office was unbroken.

Then came "Camelot," a political era well-named because it ended, in real life, as in the fictional story that created the name, with infidelity, immorality, and human misery that tarnished the memory of a president and crushed a bright hope for a period of rapid advance in human welfare and cultural enjoyment.

Was it a coincidence that the statistics on national morality began their rapid slide in the "Camelot" era, or was there a cause-and-effect relationship?

No one can say for sure, but the example set by the family in the White House is bound to have some effect on the morals of the country.

It has been demonstrated that a series of golfers in the White House—Eisenhower, Nixon and Ford—coincided with a boom in the laying out of new golf courses and the rush of millions of new golfers to buy the expensive equipment.

We have also seen that when a first lady decided it was time to beautify the country, millions of housewives, and even some husbands, took a sudden interest in planting rosebushes and setting out beds of flowers.

So it does seem to follow that a president with expensive tastes for living and sophisticated ideas about faithfulness and adultery would be likely to convey to millions of impressionable youth that his way of life was the exciting way, and that those who didn't follow it were dull personal failures who never learned how to really live.

Even before the election of 1960, which I covered, the newspapers were full of half-substantiated stories about the alleged extra-marital activities, not only of the man who was to become president, but also his father. And some of the stories were supported by photographs taken secretly by enterprising free-lance cameramen.

Actresses Marilyn Monroe and Gloria Swanson were linked by name with the son and the father in the press. But there were never any indignant denials from either the ladies or from the Kennedys, only smirks and shrugs.

Now let's go back four years to 1956. Jacqueline was a radiant mother-to-be, married to a rising and handsome young senator. Then came complications in the pregnancy, and Jackie went home to Newport, Rhode Island, where she would be near her mother. Her young husband went to the French Riviera with his father.

When Jackie lost the child, she was alone. Her husband stayed on the Riviera, though he must have known that a wife wants her husband near at a tragic moment like that.

Five years passed, years of political success and marital discord. He won the election in 1960. His wife stood by him, and was a factor in his favor because all the girls wanted to see this famous beauty, and what she was wearing. But Jackie made no speeches; her part in the campaign was purely decorative.

When they moved into the White House, the

"beautiful people" of Hollywood and the jet set moved in with them. Night-long parties were frequent. Liquor flowed freely. The youth of the country read of the parties and devoured the photographs of the happy president surrounded by his carefree friends. But Jackie took almost no part in the festivities. She spent much time in Newport and in Hyannis Port, Massachusetts, at the Kennedy Compound.

In the White House pressroom one heard rumors of nude swimming in the then-enclosed White House pool. Only the most sensational of the papers printed these stories, but they did get printed and circulated nationally.

Frequently, on the excuse of illness, Jackie avoided the White House parties. When Washington official wives received invitations to a party to be given by "the President and Mrs. Kennedy" it gradually, for some, became an occasion for regret instead of excitement. Some kept a list of valid excuses. Others attended, and spent large parts of their evenings in the elegant White House ladies' powder room, talking to each other. JFK and his wife were only rarely photographed together at these affairs. Almost invariably, it was the president and one of the "beautiful people" who graced the top-middle of the society pages the next morning. Jackie made the paper, of course, but seldom in company with her husband, and often with another handsome male friend.

Society reporters, who see all and report selectively, told their non-society colleagues that Jackie used to head for the powder room when her husband started dancing with his current favorite.

Now, before somebody else gets around to it, I'm going to put a question to myself: "Why didn't you write as frankly as this while it was going on? Why didn't you blow the whistle on Kennedy then, instead of now, fifteen or sixteen years later?"

My answer: I felt it better for the country if it *didn't* know what was happening. I thought it would do more harm than good to tell the story then. Maybe I was wrong.

My decision was influenced by a decision made by Richard Nixon in 1960. When the close-fought election was over, Nixon became convinced that he had been robbed of the presidency by ballot-box stuffing in Chicago and Texas. So, when I was invited to a Christmas party at his Washington home in December of 1960, I got him into a corner and asked him, privately, why he had not publicly protested the alleged crookedness, and taken the case to court in both states.

He looked me in the eye for a moment, and then answered, slowly and thoughtfully, "Do you think I should stand up and tell the world that the presidency of the United States can be stolen?"

Whatever Nixon may have done since, I still

believe that moment reflected a deep sense of country-before-self.

Now back to Camelot.

Things were already falling apart long before the fatal day in Dallas. There was a heavily traveled trail of broken marriages—all of them involving prominent figures of Camelot, and all given big newspaper and television play.

Among the marital casualties: the Theodore Sorensens, the Arthur Schlesingers, the Richard Goodwins, the Pierre Salingers, Jackie's sister, Lee Radziwill, a frequent party guest, and many others.

It may be understood, now, why Mrs. Kennedy was able to control herself so well after the first shock of the Dallas tragedy. To those of us who worked and watched in the White House it was plain that by the end, love had long since departed that marriage. Most other Americans of that time suspected it, too.

I believe it was Shakespeare who wrote: "The evil that men do lives after them; the good is oft interred with their bones."

This has proved true with President Kennedy. In 1976, long after his death, some of his former women friends were still coming forward with public declarations of their relationship with him. One of them, Judith Exner, shamelessly admits she was simultaneously friendly with both Kennedy and a high figure in the Mafia underworld. This, too, is not being denied.

183

And, finally, the Kennedy penchant for pretty girls has now tarnished the political name, and possibly limited the political future of his brother, Senator Ted Kennedy. The memory of Chappaquiddick would most certainly be revived and used against him if he ever tried for the presidency.

President Carter freely acknowledges that his wife, Rosalynn, has a better feel for the political sense of the country than he does. And he says he frequently adopts her ideas of what are the strongest public issues.

Reporters who covered the Carter campaign, and I was one of them, believe that it was Rosalynn's idea to make morality, or the lack of it, an issue in 1976.

Thus, in one of his earliest campaign speeches, the ex-governor of Georgia made it plain that he considered the breakdown of the family an issue at the top of his priority list.

That it did not get a lot of attention during the campaign is probably the fault of those of us in the press. To the average reporter a general breakdown of family life in America was such a broadbrush picture that it was almost impossible to concoct questions about it that would make a good political story. Much better from the viewpoint of the press, were questions that would bring forth new charges against Gerald Ford or against the Republican philosophy. The theory boiled down to "Let's you and them fight, because it makes better stories." And in the absence of specific questions, Candidate Carter didn't get a chance to go into detail on his ideas about sex, morality and marriage. But he tried. The speech, mentioned above, was one of those efforts. In it, he declared:

"The breakdown of the American family has reached extremely dangerous proportions. There can be no more urgent priority for the next administration than to see that every decision our administration makes is designed to honor and support and strengthen the American family."

In conference with Rosalynn the president has developed some ideas that he thinks will help fulfill this campaign pledge.

The emphasis on the family as a unit started on Inauguration Day, when he and Rosalynn walked, hand in hand, down Pennsylvania Avenue to the White House, with their small daughter, Amy, skipping along with them. The picture of this happy family group was a dramatic way to begin his pro-family campaign. It was not a spur-of-the-moment idea. They had planned it between them, weeks before, and had even alerted the Secret Service ten days earlier.

Then came the exhortations to his staff, his

Cabinet and to the workers in various executive departments to keep their families stable and to spend more time with their wives and children. And this was followed by the pointed suggestion to unmarried couples to get married.

When the president was advised that one of his tax revision proposals would have encouraged the trend toward unmarried couples by giving them a new tax break, Carter called the proposal back to the White House to eliminate anything that might encourage "living in sin."

One minor problem raised, especially in official Washington by the legion of unmarrieds who get party invitations, is the wording of the invitation itself, and that leads to other problems of protocol. Do you address an unmarried couple as "John Smith and guest" or "John Smith and Miss Jones" or would you write, in an effort to avoid noticing their relationship, just "Mr. Jones and Ms. Smith"? And when you address an invitation, do you write on the envelope, to "Mr. John Smith and Miss Mary Jones" and address it to the house you know they both live in? Or do you just cut them off the social list? Another problem is that many married women who are professionals in various lines use their miaden name instead of their husband's. These women are furious, and rightly so, when they get invitations sent to "Mr. Jones and Miss Smith" from social secretaries who naturally assume they are not linked by marriage.

The White House social secretary told reporters that she had laid the problem in the lap of Rosalynn Carter.

The guessing in the West Wing pressroom was that Mrs. Carter would take the sensible way out: Invite married people, and invite others as individuals, whether they live together or not. This will not eliminate those "living in sin" from the social list of the executive mansion. But it may add them to the Carters' prayer list.

Rosalynn and Jimmy Carter have put forward a few suggestions for strengthening the families of America. Rosalynn is already lobbying for some nationwide system of day-care centers for working mothers. And she thinks revival of the neighborhood school concept would be a help.

But the suggestion they put at the top of the list is that the Carter family makes its life in the White House an example of Christian living for all to see.

13

The Others

There was a chilly undertone of false courtesy in the words of the note that the Soviet Ambassador sent to the White House social secretary on a spring day in 1949. "The Ambassador of the Union of Soviet Socialist Republics regrets," it read, "that because of an unfortunate illness he will be unable to accept the kind invitation of the President and Mrs. Truman to dinner at the White House . . ." It was one of the cooler moments of the Cold War.

A former aide to President Truman reported later that the crusty Missouri-born president "blew his top" when he heard about it.

In colorful language which Truman reserved for occasions of extreme provocation, in spite of his Baptist upbringing, he roared his displeasure

189

in an ear-searing phone call to the State Department.

"He's a liar!" Truman snapped. "That (deleted) slimey character is no sicker than I am, and I'm in perfect health. He has lied to me for the last time, and this time he was insulted my wife, to boot. I want him recalled to Moscow! And I want you to say you are doing it because he insulted the wife of the president!"

There was a polite "Yes, sir" on the other end of the line, as the president hung up and stomped out of his office back toward the residential quarters.

But diplomats are masters of the art of avoiding embarrassment, and before the president made it through the long hallways and up the stairs to relay the news to First Lady Bess Truman, a fast phone call from the State Department, by Secretary of State Dean Acheson, had already informed her of her husband's rage and advised a quiet talk to cool him off.

And Bess Truman—a first lady whose influence on her husband was so much like the influence now wielded by First Lady Rosalynn Carter—responded with great effect, and thus ended a diplomatic incident that might have made the Cold War a lot colder.

As a White House correspondent most of the last thirty-seven years, I have watched first ladies "do their thing" as far back as 1940, toward the end of FDR's second term. They all faced the same tasks and essentially the same problems. They all met their responsibilities in different ways. But of all the first ladies during this time—and there were seven—Bess Truman came the closest to what is now becoming known as "the Rosalynn Factor" in the White House.

Like Rosalynn Carter, Mrs. Truman was a down-to-earth person, with simple tastes and a direct manner of expressing herself. And, like the relationship between Jimmy Carter and his wife, the president listened, and usually heeded her advice when Bess felt strongly enough about something to speak to him about it.

Like Rosalynn, Bess was consulted regularly by the president on political and governmental matters, and former Truman staffers say that historians will never know how many of the president's important decisions were decisively influenced by the lady who was his administrative assistant in the Senate even before he was elevated to the vice presidency.

Mrs. Truman, now ninety-two years old and troubled with arthritis, shows signs of setting a new longevity record for the line of hard-working women who shared their husbands' terms as president over the last two hundred years.

Lady Bird Johnson was another who came close

to the Rosalynn pattern. She campaigned effectively in her husband's 1964 bid for the presidency. Like the current first lady, Mrs. Johnson did a lot of the campaigning on her own. Since there was no Federal Election Law to curb the spending in those days, Lady Bird was financially able to storm the Southern states in her own private train, "The Lady Bird Special," while her husband toured other parts of the country by plane.

Where Lady Bird and Rosalynn part company is in the kinds of projects they chose. Mrs. Johnson espoused the cause of beautifying America, and she prodded her husband into preparing a Highway Beautification Act that was passed by Congress in 1965, and is known to this day as "The Lady Bird Act."

Lady Bird planted trees and bulbs, dedicated parks and gardens, made endless appearances to beat the drums for conservation of natural resources as well as national beauty, and even toured river valleys by raft to draw attention to areas in need of official protection.

Still active and healthy at sixty-four, Lady Bird came back into politics in 1977 to help her son-in-law, Charles Robb, and daughter, Lynda, make it to the first rung of the political ladder in their successful campaign for the nomination to be lieutenant governor of the state of Virginia. When reporters asked her why she had chosen to abandon the usual grandmotherly campaign baby-sitting chore for action on the rugged campaign trail, she gave an answer that sounds now like an echo of things that Rosalynn Carter has been saying since she entered the White House, "You simply want to do what you can."

Jacqueline Kennedy Onassis was a first lady poured in a completely different mold from any other of this century. She was, first of all, only thirty-one years old when President Kennedy was inaugurated. Although there was about as much interest in her as there was in her handsome young husband while they were in the White House, the interest centered in such things as her bouffant hairdo—which was copied by hundreds of thousands of young American girls—her pillbox hats, which also became a national fad, and her varying styles of fashionable dress.

There was nothing in her background of experience to suggest that Jacqueline assisted the president in substantive matters, but she was a beautiful hostess, and the elegant parties of the "Camelot" era in the White House are still remembered with nostalgia by the Washington social set.

Mrs. Kennedy, probably in part because of her youth, was quiet, even shy, in public and seldom did any public speaking.

I watched her in a campaign television interview during the West Virginia primary of 1960, the campaign in which Kennedy later started the "great debate" tradition by challenging Hubert Humphrey to an inconclusive contest in the capital city, Charleston. Her extreme reticence on that TV show so provoked the newsman who was questioning her that—after a series of one-word replies to his much-longer questions—he just gave up the effort and blurted out: "Mrs. Kennedy, you aren't very talkative, are you!"

After that embarrassment, interviews were eliminated from her schedule, and she rode along with the candidate because Kennedy and his aides knew that the crowds wanted to see her, and see what she was wearing.

Mamie Eisenhower, who suffered an attack of rheumatic fever when she was a child, had to be careful of her health, so her activities as the first lady were centered mainly on greeting many thousands of guests at the White House during her eight years there.

Mamie refused to go along with the Women's Lib movement, and it was her custom, even before Ike was elected president, always to put her husband in the spotlight, and to stay in the shadows herself, as much as possible.

The ladies of the country made "Mamie Bangs"

a nationwide trend in the beauty parlors, and the "Mamie Pink" of her dresses and her household decor also developed almost in a nationwide fad.

Long before she entered the White House she was a veteran in the art of entertaining. Her chief innovation in White House entertaining was the creation of the E-shaped table which made it possible for her to sit beside the president at state affairs.

Her son, John, wrote of his mother: "She could more than hold her own with him in private—her frail health belied the strength of her will."

In the face of rumors that her husband had been unfaithful during the war in Europe, Mamie was always by his side, and never uttered a word about the stories publicly. Even now, she makes a sentimental journey once a year from her farm in Gettysburg to visit the Eisenhower tomb and library in Abilene, Kansas. Secret service agents, who still protect her, do the driving. Mamie is now eighty years old, highly respected by Americans who lived in the Eisenhower years.

Patricia Nixon is a first lady whose years in the White House brought both triumph and bitter defeat. There was praise for the Nixon accomplishment in foreign affaris—for opening the doors of China and blunting the sharp-edged rhetoric of the Cold War by initiating

Soviet-American detente—and disgrace for the scandals which made Nixon the first president to resign and hand over affairs of state to the vice president. Pat Nixon weathered it all and went into retirement with her public image untarnished by her husband's troubles.

Mrs. Nixon was well prepared for her role as first lady. She had eight years as the "second lady," as wife of the vice president, in which to learn the ropes. Thus she shared with Rosalynn Carter the advantage of previous experience.

Though quiet, by nature, and a very private person, Pat Nixon seemed more at ease when meeting people than her husband, who throughout his career, was more at ease before a crowd of ten thousand than he was when faced with the task of making small talk with one individual.

As first lady she espoused the causes of volunteerism and community service. And during the Nixon first term she did a lot of traveling on her own to publicize these projects. Unfortunately, she seemed always ill at ease when talking to reporters, and this tended to reduce the time allotted to interviews, and cut down the publicity she sought for her work.

In the course of her eight years as "second lady" and nearly six years in the White House, Pat Nixon traveled in some eighty countries, and her face and her gracious manner, and her obvious love for children, made her one of the better known and most loved of the wives of presidents.

When Nixon was finally forced from office, there was a worldwide wave of sympathy for the quiet lady who was banished with him.

Betty Ford had something less than three years to make her mark as the first lady, and she was handicapped through that time by crippling illnesses—first chronic trouble with a pinched nerve in her neck, and then a frightening operation to remove a breast. But she made her mark in spite of it all, first as the highest ranking proponent of the Equal Rights Amendment and Women's Lib, and second, as a lady unafraid of speaking her mind, whether the voters of the country were on her side, or not.

To any who followed her career closely in the White House, as I did, it is pretty obvious that Betty Ford and the First Lady who succeeded her, Rosalynn Carter, were poles apart in their opinions on many important issues.

The Fords, although lifelong members of the Episcopal Church, and though the president was reported to be a close friend and confidant of Evangelist Billy Zeoli, attended church services only infrequently during their White House tenure. They were what might be called "closet Christians." And when questioned during the

197

Ford-Carter campaign about their religion, they always made a special point of commenting that they did not "wear their religion on their sleeves," leaving the impression that they thought Carter did.

In fairness, it must be reported that President Ford, in the early days of his administration, took part in early morning prayer sessions at the White House once a week, with some of his Christian friends in Congress, including the man who succeeded him as leader of Republicans in the House, Congressman John Rhodes of Arizona, and Congressman Albert Quie of Minnesota, a leader in the congressional prayer and Bible study movement.

Rhodes and Quie confirm, however, that the early morning prayer sessions became less frequent as the Fords plunged deeper into their duties, and finally were suspended altogether until shortly before the 1976 campaign got under way.

Betty Ford, meanwhile, was gaining a reputation as being frank and outspoken in her comments on everything from sex to the arts.

One such incident was the now well-remembered exchange between First Lady Ford and a newsman on the subject of premarital sex.

Asked what would be her reaction if her daughter came to her and confessed that she was having an affair, Mrs. Ford replied: "I wouldn't be surprised."

When the same question was put to Rosalynn Carter some months later, the current first lady's answer was: "I would be shocked. But, of course, my daughter is only ten years old."

Mrs. Ford, who was a dancer and theatrical performer before her marriage to Gerald Ford, doesn't say much in public about her religion, even though one of her sons is a seminary graduate and now an active clergyman.

In sharp contrast, the public statements and hundreds of speeches delivered by Mrs. Carter are laced with references to the Holy Spirit, to the need for constant prayer for the Lord's guidance, and to the long history of devout Christian faith in her family, and the family of her husband. One reason for this difference between the two first ladies may be the Southern tradition of talking more openly about spiritual things.

A Republican officeholder commented that the lack of public comment about religion by the Fords does not indicate any lesser degree of religious faith. It is a reflection, rather, of the lifelong belief of the Ford family that public displays of religious faith amount to using religion for political purposes.

First Lady Ford's candor about things other than the spiritual did make her a popular figure, especially during the election of 1976, and the primaries of that spring.

Buttons began appearing all over the country urging: "Betty Ford's Husband For President," and the president never failed to get a laugh from his audience when he ruefully remarked: "Betty's standings in the polls are higher than mine."

A good part of Betty's popularity stemmed from her brave willingness to brush aside the taboo against discussing breast operations in public, and her repeated public assurances to women that they should not fear to be examined for breast cancer, because early detection is the key to survival.

Cancer researchers have said that her open talk about her own operation probably saved the lives of unnumbered women who faced the same frightening decision.

There is one way in which Betty and Rosalynn were as alike as twins. Neither one ever hesitated to take a public stand in opposition to the views of their respective husbands, without fear of the political impact. In addition, both of them worked for the alleviation of mental handicaps; Betty Ford for retarded children and Rosalynn Carter for better help for the mentally ill.

Eleanor Roosevelt, the wife of Franklin D. Roosevelt, had more than thirteen years in the White House and consequently probably will be remembered always as the first lady who pioneered the modern image of a typical active president's wife.

While giving strong support to her husband's New Deal efforts to bring the country out of the Depression, Mrs. Roosevelt was the one who created the idea of an independent office of the first lady, with its own programs, designed to dovetail with the programs the administration was pushing.

Eleanor also served as FDR's scout, and prowled the big city ghettos and the Midwest dust bowls, looking for places where federal help was needed and reporting them to the president when she found them.

Though her speaking voice was not the best, she was in constant demand as a speaker, and was constantly scheduling her time to capacity. Her interests were so varied and her life so full that she finally accepted the offer to write a syndicated newspaper column, called "My Day," so the women of the country would know what she was doing. The column became so popular that she continued writing it long after the death of her husband.

But a personal tragedy hung over the whole career of this hard-working, brilliant first lady. There were rumors, first, and then there was factual proof of marital infidelity by her husband. And her children launched a parade of marriages and divorces that raised questions in the minds of many Christians about the wisdom of a First Lady who worked so hard for the welfare of the country's poor, while her own family was falling apart.

So, there they are: seven first ladies, each with a different view of what she could most effectively accomplish while her husband was president.

Now comes First Lady Rosalynn Carter, the first to declare openly that Jesus Christ will reside in the White House so long as the Carters do.

Many Christians believe that the Lord's timing of the Carter takeover was not without purpose, and offers a great potential for good.

With the American family on the decline, what could be better for the nation than to have the close-knit, God-fearing Carters in the White House, a living example of what a family could and should be?

With the nation's divorce rate climbing, how fortunate to have in the White House a president who says that after thirty-one years of marriage, his wife, Rosalynn, is the only woman he has ever loved.

Finally, with the nation slipping morally, and the idea growing that it is not necessary for men and women to marry in order to live together, how refreshing it is to have a president with the guts to exhort people in government who are "living in sin" to "get married."

And how good it is to have our chief executive stand before a press conference, heavily weighted with cynics, and tell them frankly his Christian view of promiscuity and what he would do about it.

The president said, "My preference is that those who associate with me—in fact, all people—would honor the same standards that I honor. But I've never held it against people who had a different stand from myself.

"I've done everything I could, properly and legitimately, to encourage my staff members' families to be stable, and I have also encouraged the same sort of thing in my Cabinet.

"If there are some who have slipped from grace, then I can only say that I'll do the best I can to forgive them, and pray for them."

But now that the president is becoming more and more engrossed in guiding the secular affairs of the country and supervising our foreign relations, the Christian community of Washington has turned to a new subject for special prayer. It is praying that First Lady Rosalynn Carter will see that one of her most important jobs is to make sure this unique opportunity for Christian witnessing by a family in the White House will not be lost.

14

The Woman

"I am determined that the White House will be a place that people can turn to for help." That is Rosalynn Carter's view of her job as first lady—and she is a first lady with ideas of her own, who frankly admits that she argues with the president when she thinks he is wrong, and then adds, modestly: "I think sometimes I win."

She is a first lady who says she intends to entertain less and work more. And her friends seem to be in agreement that when Rosalynn puts her mind to it, "less usually turns out to be 'more.'"

Mrs. Carter is more reticent than her husband. She doesn't talk as openly or as much about her religious faith. That may be because the press doesn't ask her about it as often as they do her husband. But when asked, she readily confesses that she was "born again" in mid-life, just like Jimmy, and that the experience gives her the same feeling of inner strength and support that he describes.

Her Washington pastor, the Rev. Dr. Charles A. Trentham of the First Baptist Church, who has become a personal friend since their move to the capital, says that "her depth of faith and her commitment to Jesus Christ is certainly commensurate to that of her husband." He adds that "when the Bible lessons are discussed in the Sunday school, she responds in a dialogue that reflects a deep and comprehensive knowledge of the Scriptures."

Dr. Trentham says that Mrs. Carter's primary religious concern is directed toward "the broken people of society, and that is where religion is translated into the practical, and where the depth of compassion is revealed."

Rosalynn herself believes that she developed "the closest relationship with Jesus Christ when Jimmy was governor. You can go for a long time thinking you can solve all your problems, then suddenly you realize you can't do it, and you call on God for help. I had a lot of pressures back then, a suddenly completely different life. I think I finally reached the point where I realized I couldn't do everything I thought I had to do. When that happened, I realized I was not perfect, but I knew that the Lord didn't expect me to be. I try to keep this in mind, now, and I function better."

Her husband often asks her what she thinks about whatever he happens to be working on at the moment, but she adds that she frequently gives him her opinion without waiting to be asked. "And the family talks about the issues when we get together," she says. Whether or not she plays the role of policy adviser depends on the issue, she explains. The president always comes to her for advice on matters concerning health, help for the elderly, betterment of care for the mentally ill and various welfare improvements. She also consults with him on things in the field of education, and one of her newest projects is a plan to reach residents of the various big city ghettos and see to it that they get the kind of education and training that will steer them away from the wasted lives that they are headed toward.

"Jimmy always wants to know how I feel about an important appointment before he announces it," she says. She adds that she joined the president in the decision go give Walter Mondale second place on the Democratic ticket. She did it, she says, only after careful inquiry disclosed that Mrs. Mondale was an active, intelligent cheerful woman who would be an ideal choice to help her in the work of the first lady.

What troubled Mrs. Carter at first was the

feeling of being fenced in at the White House, the feeling of not being free to "run down to the store and buy a loaf of bread" or to ask Jimmy to "put on your denim jacket and take Amy to McDonalds."

The first lady is very much aware of the constant threat of assassination. If she should forget it, the secret service agents are always there to remind her.

"Naturally, it concerns me," she says, but you kind of keep it in the back of your mind, you just try not to dwell on it."

The impact on daughter Amy of a life constantly in the limelight is another matter of concern, but not a present concern. "Right now I don't think it's bad for her. I don't think it's doing her any harm, because she's so completely nonchalant. But I do worry sometimes about what will happen when she's older."

The first lady admits to some slight resentment over all the attention given to what she wears. She has always had a "sensible" taste in clothes; neat, trim and attractive, but not glamorous. She's sorry if this disappoints the high-fashion people, but that's the way she is. And she was adamant on the decision to bring her own sewing machine to the White House from Plains, but admits now there haven't been many opportunities to use it.

She gets suddenly defensive when someone makes remarks about the president carrying his own luggage. "If Jimmy wants to carry his luggage

I think he can," she says. "And if some people think that's an artificial thing, just to create an image—well, they just don't know Jimmy.

She likes informality at her parties, but she was never one to give a lot of parties. Mrs. Carter once coaxed her husband into joining her in square dance lessons and one of the plans that she keeps "on the back burner" is to put on a big old-fashioned square dance in the White House East Room.

That big and highly successful outdoor picnic on the South Lawn on July 20, 1977 was typical of the First Lady's idea of "real fun." It was a party for congressmen and their families, and the heat on that date was in the high nineties, but people were having such a good time that even the cynics of the press agree that they didn't seem to be noticing the heat. There was volleyball and square dancing and a lot of other country-type fun, and when somebody suggested to the president that this might be the first party of that kind since the days of Andrew Jackson, the president laughed and replied: "I really would have like to have been at that one, too."

Incidentally, he stayed, in spite of the heat and the crush for almost two hours, instead of the fifteen minutes he customarily gives to such functions. And one of his first acts at the picnic was to "free the press" who had been ushered to a roped-in enclosure where they could stand and watch the fun. The president untied the rope and sent them running.

The first lady says she supports the Equal Rights Amendment to the Constitution, and has done a little long-distance telephone lobbying when it came to a vote in some state legislatures. In fact, she is credited with convincing a key member of the Indiana legislature to change his vote and break a tie in favor of the amendment.

"It means equal pay for an equal job done," she argues, "and I know of so many women in Georgia, as there are everywhere, who are the sole supporters of their families. ERA would help them."

One the issue of abortion, she stands with Jimmy. "I personally don't like abortion," she says, "but I am not for an amendment to the Constitution to make it illegal, because I've seen what happens when abortion was made illegal in some states. Abortion mills spring up in neighboring states where it is legal. We should try to prevent the need for abortion, by pushing for organized family planning, better sex education and less red tape in the adoption procedures."

She points out that when her husband was governor of Georgia he took her advice and set up a family planning clinic in every one of the state's 159 counties. Within two years, she says, use of the clinics grew by 200 percent.

Rosalynn stiffens at any criticism of the family's

decision to bring to the White House from her Georgia prison Mary Fitzpatrick, a paroled murderer.

"We got a lot of mail about it, but so many of those people just didn't understand. Mary's really a good person. She was with us in the mansion in Atlanta and she could do anything. She took care of Amy from the time Amy was three until she was seven, and she also cooked, cleaned and greeted guests at the door—and just everything. It's fun to have her back. She's like a member of the family and she and Amy love each other dearly."

The first lady admits she doesn't get up as early in the morning now as she used to.

"Jimmy goes over to his office at seven," she says, "but Amy doesn't leave for school until 8:30, so I wait and eat breakfast with her. The rest of the day I work on things like my projects for mental health, or for the elderly, or I plan receptions for our foreign visitors, or write letters. There's always something to do, and usually too much, and one of the hardest jobs I have is to decide my priorities. There are so many good causes that I just don't have time for. But I realize I can help by just lending my name."

Mrs. Carter and her East Wing office are responsible for all the functions that go on in the White House, whether it is one of the first lady's projects or not—whether it's a breakfast to be given by the president for members of Congress or a working dinner for a foreign head of state or a visit by some of the people who helped the Carters during the campaign.

She has not only a paid staff of eighteen, but there are usually a half-dozen volunteers who come in every day to answer phones for her, to type or do other chores. The first lady explains that she gets forty to fifty invitations every day "and somebody has to answer them."

Mrs. Carter says the thing she likes best about being the "head lady" at the White House is the opportunity it gives her to meet people. Not just the great and the powerful and the famous, but ordinary people who come to dinners and receptions and most of whom turn out to be so genuinely nice. "I just love them all."

Among the most interesting guests she has had at the White House, she says was a couple who run a grocery store in North Carolina. The couple gave the Carters some help during the campaign, were promised an invitation to the White House, and they got it promptly—an invitation to one of the first of the Carter state dinners. They told her the experience was something they would cherish all of their days.

One of the big things she is working on, in her view, is what she and Jimmy call the "Friendship Force." What it amounts to is a friendly exchange of people between countries. They started it when he was governor, with an exchange of two hundred people between Georgia and Brazil. "That was in 1973," she thinks, and she said it was a terrific success. "They paid their way and we paid our way, and the Georgians have been doing it every year since. When you get acquainted like this and make a lot of permanent friends in another country you get interested in that country," she explained. "Now, anything that happens in Brazil is important to us, because we have so many friends there."

On one of the trips to Brazil, she recalls, Jimmy preached in a church there.

Rosalynn Carter has been such a busy first lady that, after nearly seven months in the White House she had never made a downstairs tour of the house, the tour that the tourists take. So she set aside a couple of hours and had the Committee for the Preservation of the White House show her around the lower floor of her own new home. Her explorations had been confined to the warehouse where the furnishings used by other presidents were stored.

"It's awesome to me," she declares, "just to see it and to say 'This was Harry Truman's chest of drawers, this was Theodore Roosevelt's bed—' "

Having tackled the Spanish language with enthusiasm and won a battle to make her memory retain enough for simple conversations, Rosalynn now vows that her next project is to study French "so we can use it when we visit our friends in

213

Europe."

So far, when Jimmy has talked of plans for trips abroad, Rosalynn has invariably found some important project on her schedule. And besides, she explains, she doesn't like to leave Amy behind, and doesn't want to take her out of school, either.

Dr. Trentham, the family's Washington pastor, says that he thinks Mrs. Carter is looking "a little weary" and he has gently suggested she might like to slow down a bit. But he says she has, since joining his church, taken an active interest in several of the church's programs for the poor and broken, in addition to the ones she supervises from the White House.

"She has expressed deep interest in our home mission program which we call 'Bread for the City,' he said. "In this effort we try to supplement the income of people living on diminishing retirement income, and we also look to their medical needs.

"She is also giving support to our 'cheer-up club' for out-patients of St. Elizabeth's [mental] hospital. We bring about twenty-five of them to the church every Tuesday morning, give them a good lunch, and then an afternoon of music and other entertainment, and craft work."

Of all her projects, Dr. Trentham thinks the first lady is most deeply committed to the human rights policy which her husband is preaching to all the nations of the world.

Mrs. Carter just shrugs and brushes off questioners who wonder how she stands "the pressures" of life at the pinnacle of national politics and government.

"They don't even compare to what you have to endure from opponnets in state and local politics," says the former first lady of Georgia. "After you have lived with Lester Maddox [former segregated-restaurant-owner-turned-governor who was lieutenant governor during Carter's four years as governor] nothing can bother you any more." Maddox was and still is an all-out political foe of the president who made a personal foray into the north during the campaign to follow the president around and declare Carter was not telling the truth about what he did in Georgia.

One of the most frequent questions asked of Mrs. Carter is "Why do you refuse to serve liquor in the White House?"

Her standard reply: "Because I don't want to."

She also gets a lot of questions about her secret of keeping herself looking so fresh and young, despite the rigors of a campaign that started nearly four years before election day, and picked up a furious momentum near the close.

She has been asked whether she has ever had her face lifted.

The answer is "sort of." But the face lift that Mrs. Carter had was a surgical necessity and not

215

merely a matter of cosmetics.

White House Press Secretary Jody Powell finally relieved her of this question by giving the official answer to the press.

Mrs. Carter was suffering from what the doctors call a "congenital blepharism" which is a spasm affecting the eyelids, so that they involuntarily close down frequently and unexpectedly. So Mrs. Carter took her doctor's advice and had a surgeon perform a "blepharoplasty," an operation in which wrinkles, bagging around the eyes, and saggy skin are removed. The result, though it may not be the primary purpose of the operation, is to restore a youthful appearance to the face. So the answer to the question about the face lift is still "sort of."

Mrs. Carter is a lady with firm opinions on many subjects. She believes that women should work outside the home if they are able. Why? Because she thinks they would be happier, and there would be fewer broken marriages, if more women could honestly feel that they were contributing something, to the home or to the general welfare of society.

"I know it would have been very hard for me to take if Jimmy had been out doing great things, and I had stayed at home. I feel secure, I think, because I have always been doing what Jimmy was doing."

When she finds that there is something she

needs to know how to do, Mrs. Carter doesn't hesitate. She goes to the nearest available expert and finds out how to do it.

When she first entered the Georgia governor's mansion as the wife of the governor she was faced with a maze of protocol decisions and she didn't even know how to set a table properly. So she promptly found an expert—the wife of the German consul in Atlanta, who had even written books on gracious entertaining, and got a quick course in table setting and protocol. And as a bonus, Rosalynn also learned some gourmet cooking, and collected a full set of the special cookware that it takes to be a success at it.

Rosalynn Carter doesn't like to "waste time" at fashion and furniture shows or listening to lectures on food. Some of her friends think that may be the reason why the first lady never acquired a large roster of close friends. She always had serious work to do and never had time for the social things.

Unlike her husband, the first lady says she finds little time for reading, despite the time she spends on brushing up her speed-reading skills. What reading she does usually is concentrated on "issue papers" or studies of the various programs in which she is interested.

Although she is soft-spoken about personal matters, she declares: "I have very strong opinions about almost everything, and I always let Jimmy know how I feel, even though he disagrees and doesn't react well to my viewpoint."

Jody Powell echoes her sentiments on this. "People tend to underestimate her because she talks so softly and with that Southern accent. But if you've ever been on the opposite side of a dispute with her, you've made a very serious mistake," he says.

Rosalynn also lets it be known that she doesn't think Jimmy deserves all the credit for getting elected president. To her way of thinking, she and the family played an important part in the victory.

"We've always worked together on everything, and we have always shared a tremendous sense of accomplishment," she says. Her husband doesn't argue with her about this. He is the first to give his wife full credit.

When Rosalynn was a school girl, some thirty-five years ago, her toughest subject was social studies. She used to get up at five o'clock in the morning to master her lessons before going to school. Throughout her life, she says, she has always tried to work hardest at her weakest subject. Now, as first lady in the White House, her early morning work on social studies has served her well. She now oversees half a dozen vast social programs designed to touch all fifty states.

The first lady also is one who does not hesitate in making hard decisions.

In April, 1977, in a routine medical checkup,

the doctor discovered a lump in one of her breasts. Without hesitation she agreed to have the lump removed immediately. The biopsy showed, fortunately, that it was benign.

But the very morning after the surgery, Rosalynn refused to cancel her usual Spanish lesson, and later the same day attended a lecture and a concert at the Kennedy Center.

Her family noted, however, that before going into surgery she insisted on calling her mother, Allie Smith, in Plains so that the mother would not hear about it first on the radio, and be worried.

And after it was all over Rosalynn made good use of the experience, publicly advising all women that "the best thing you can do is to have a breast examination and, if necessary, have something done about it at once. That's what I did," she added, "and if I hadn't done it I would have worried needlessly."

Rosalynn doesn't enjoy shopping for clothes for herself, according to her lifelong "best friend," Ruth Carter Stapleton, the president's evangelist sister.

She recalls that on one occasion when she went shopping especially to help the first lady pick out some new things for herself, Rosalynn seemed more concerned with finding something for Ruth. "That's typical of her," Ruth commented, "always thinking of others."

In the spring of 1977, after they had moved to

Washington, the son of one of her lifelong friends, Barbara Thomas, was critically hurt in an automobile accident in Georgia. The boy lingered in a coma before dying, and all through that period, Rosalynn called repeatedly from Washington. "I couldn't talk to anyone but Rosalynn," the mother commented later.

Rosalynn Smith Carter was born on August 18, 1927, the year that Charles Lindbergh first flew the Atlantic non-stop. It was the beginning of an era of great and inspiring deeds by brave and ambitious people. Something of the spirit of her birth year must have stuck with Mrs. Carter, to bring her from a home on the wrong side of the tracks to the summit of power in only a half century of life.

But she is still not satisfied with herself. The first lady is still bent on self-improvement. She still springs to attention every time she hears of something new that she would like to learn about.

"I'm a very impatient person," she says. "I don't know what it is that makes me lose my patience so often, but I do. Jimmy always listens to what is bothering me, and that helps."

A friend, who has known the first lady since she was a child, put in this suggestion: "I think I know why Rosalynn is so impatient. It's because she wants to do so much while she is first lady, and there are only four years—or eight at the most—in which to do it."